# Advanced Custom Paint Techniques

1310 Sunny Slope Lane
Stillwater, MN 55082
http://www.wolfgangpublications.com

1

# Legals

First published in 2003 by Wolfgang Publications Inc.,
1310 Sunny Slope Lane, Stillwater MN 55082

ISBN number: 1-929133-14-6

Printed and bound in the USA

# Advanced Custom Painting Techniques

# From the Publisher

I am very pleased to be part of another great Jon Kosmoski book. The best part of working with Jon is the fact that he doesn't know the meaning of the phrase, "burn out." I didn't know Jon in high school, but his enthusiasm for each project, each new product and each new idea is as genuine and contagious as that exhibited by any sixteen year old.

The hard part of working with Jon Kosmoski is the simple challenge of trying to keep up. The high school analogy applies once again. Though he's well past high school age, he still hits it hard every day. He ought to be retiring, instead he's adding on to the garage and putting a down payment on a steel Deuce roadster body. Jon takes pride not just in his work but in the amount of work he gets done each day. This is a man who still works hard, works fast, and hates to wait for anyone.

I have to thank Jon for those occasions when I did get him to slow down, or even stop, so I could take a photo, or take the same photo again. And though most of the photos are mine, I need to thank Jon's long-time partner, Pat Kosmoski, for taking photos when I couldn't get to the shop.

Timothy Remus

# Introduction

The world of custom painting has changed tremendously in just the past few years. New products make it easier and easier to get a particular effect. New metallic base coats, color-change pigments, kandies and pearls mean you can do beautiful paint jobs and complex layouts with an ease unheard of just a few years ago.

These new products don't apply themselves though. You still need to follow the principles of good custom painting. In fact, the only way to get the best results from all these new products is with the correct application techniques. In my seminars I still see painters who haven't learned to walk the car, or keep the cap parallel to the surface, or use an invisible grid to keep the amount of overlap between each pass exactly the same for the entire vehicle.

This book takes you into my shop as we do four complete start-to-finish paint jobs. These jobs on both bikes and cars use a variety of the new paint products. By using hundreds of color photos we've tried to show you exactly what I've learned in 47 years of custom painting. The sequences cover panel preparation as well

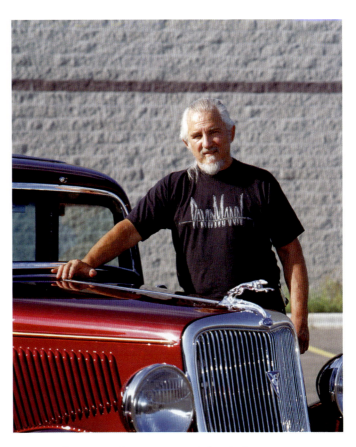

as the actual painting. That's because you can't talk about custom painting without talking about the preparation.

With custom painting there are no limits and no rules. You can mix your own color, change the effect of a kandy job by changing the basecoat, or create a layout limited only by your imagination. There's nothing as satisfying as looking at a beautiful car or bike and being able to say, "I did that paint job."

# Chapter One

# Your Shop

## A Shop that's Clean, Safe and Efficient

When it comes to your shop, you need a space where you can get work done in a safe, efficient way. You need dust control and air movement for painting, a means of heating the shop and a source of clean, compressed air.

I can't say enough about the importance of a good, clean air supply. You can't do a quality paint job if you're always waiting for the compressor to catch up, or there's water and other contaminants in the airstream. A good air supply starts

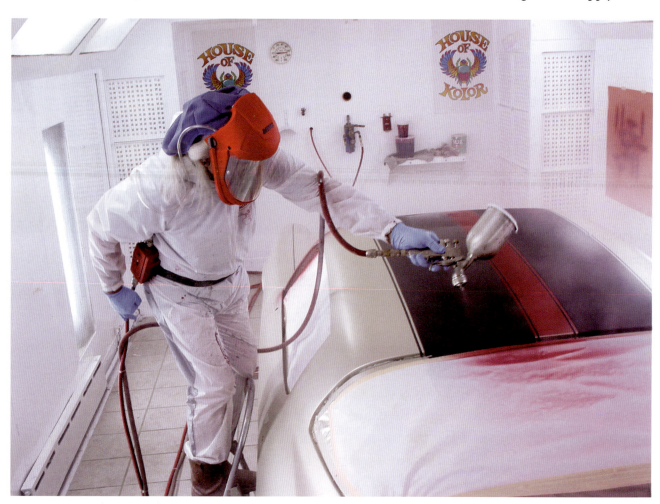

*Whether it's your power tools, the spray gun or the fresh-air hood, you need clean dry air and lots of it. Power tools need dry air, the spray gun needs clean dry air so you don't have any contaminants or water in the air that carries the paint, and the hood needs specially filtered breathable air.*

with a big enough air compressor.

## COMPRESSORS

When it comes to spray painting, the minimum compressor you should use in today's world with the HVLP guns is a five horse, two-stage unit with a minimum 60 gallon air tank. The new guns are HVLP and use high volumes of air, more so than an old-style paint gun. But the best feature of that technology is that it reduces over spray so there's less hazard for the painter using the HVLP guns and that includes primer and anything else you're going to do. Less over spray also means you use less material.

The next most important thing for trouble free painting is to set up the air system properly. Generally you need a minimum of 20 feet of pipe running away from the compressor and you want to put a flexible line between the compressor and that line. These flexible lines are available from a number of places but WW Grainger is one that sells them and they'll handle 500 psi. This way the shake of the compressor is never going to knock your piping off the wall, which happened to me one time (you learn everything the hard way).

For feeder lines I would say use a minimum 3/4 inch and then drop to1/2 inch and always pull the feeders

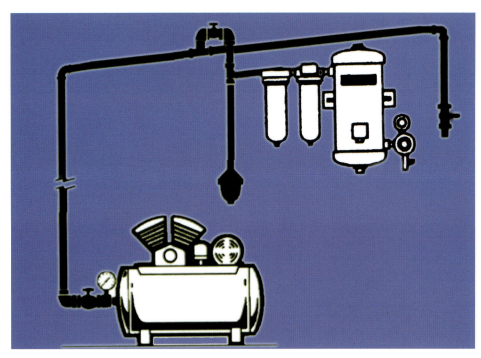

*You need to think about the compressor and air distribution system. Feeder lines need to turn up, then down, each line needs a shut off valve and clean out plug.*

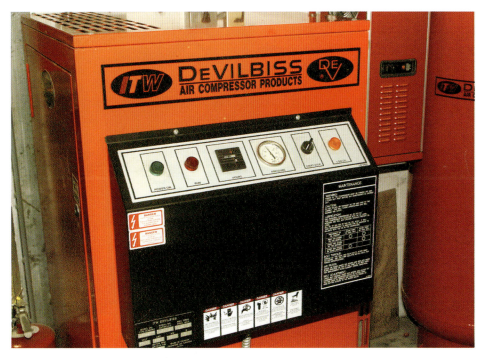

*In my shop, the air line that feeds the booth runs off this 10 horsepower super silent compressor from DeVilbiss.*

7

*Between the compressor and the spray gun I use this DAD 500 multi-stage filtering system. Left to right, there's a water/oil/dirt filter, a coalescer to remove oil aerosols and more dirt, and a desiccant to trap water vapor.*

*When it comes to feeding the spray gun, the 5/16 inch hose and standard quick-connector fittings just aren't good enough. Today you need 3/8 inch hose and the bigger fittings seen on the left.*

off the top of the main run and then bring them down. You can do that with a T facing towards the ceiling and two street 90s. I like to put a ball valve in there for a shut off at each drop so that I can service the regulator or deal with a maintenance problem without bleeding the entire system.

## CLEAN AIR

A regulator with a water trap will help get moisture out of the air but nothing works better than either a membrane dryer or a desiccant dryer so you will be positively assured that there is no moisture in your air that will eat up your air tools. More important, water in the system will put moisture in the paint job, it will mix into the paint which can cause blistering, bubbling and delamination.

Of course with reciprocating compressors oil molecules get mixed into the air which these dryers also help to eliminate.

A final filter at the booth is a good idea too. A micron filter where the air supply hits the booth. I do that so it takes any particles flying in the air and gets them out of the air so they don't mix into your paint job. With that kind of a setup you're off to a very good start.

## THE HOSE

It's important with an HVLP gun to use the proper size hose and what all the manufactures are recommending is a 3/8 inch hose with the special fittings that are double the area of the normal 5/16 inch fitting. This way there is almost no pressure drop. If you use 40 feet of hose in the booth with 5/16 inch hose the pressure drop can be substantial. Using the new fittings and bigger hose you will have little or no pressure drop, maybe one or two lbs. at the gun. So for air equipment and anything else you are doing in the shop you may as well just buy the 3/8 inch hose. Be sure to get a hose that's designed for spraying so it doesn't come apart on the inside and cause you trouble later.

When the people from Sharpe spray guns get a complaint, the first thing they do is put a little device on the end of the air line that has a very small paper filter. They put that on and they just run the air through it for about a half hour at a low pace like 30 to 40 psi. Then they take it apart and examine the gauze with a magnifying glass and they can tell the condition of the air that feeds the spray guns. Eighty percent of the time they trace the painting problems to contaminates within the air system. So in other words, the actual air that the man is working with is causing his problems.

You don't want more hose in the booth than you need. The hose should drop down to the floor and get all the way around the car and

## Pressure Loss with 100 psi Inlet Pressure

| | 35' HOSE | | 50' HOSE | |
|---|---|---|---|---|
| | 15 CFM | 25 CFM | 15 CFM | 25 CFM |
| 1/4" ID | 35 psi | 87 psi | 50 psi | * |
| 5/16" ID | 12.6 psi | 31.5 psi | 18 psi | 45 psi |
| 3/8" ID | 4.2 psi | 10.5 psi | 6 psi | 15 psi |

*Here's an example of the kinds of pressure drop you will experience when using hoses of too small a diameter.*

## Minimum Pipe Size Recommendations

| Compressor Size | Compressor Capacity | Main Air Line | Min. Pipe Diameter |
|---|---|---|---|
| 1-1/2 & 2 HP | 6 to 9 CFM | Over 50 ft. | 3/4" |
| 3 & 5 HP | 12 to 20 CFM | Up to 200 ft. | 3/4" |
| | | Over 200 ft. | 1" |
| 5 to 10 HP | 2 to 40 CFM | Up to 100 ft. | 3/4" |
| | | 100 to 200 ft. | 1-1/4" |
| | | Over 200 ft. | 1-1/4" |
| 10 to 15 HP | 40 to 60 CFM | Up to 100 ft. | 1" |
| | | 100 to 200 ft. | 1-1/4" |
| | | Over 200 ft. | 1-1/2" |

* Under no circumstances are we advising that correct air line piping reduces contaminants so much that you do not need a filtering system. A point of use filter is still strongly recommended.

*The bigger the compressor, and the longer the main feed line, the bigger the pipe diameter needs to be. DeVilbiss*

*A good spray booth provides dust control with good lighting. Booths come in a variety of cross-draft and side draft models. Many offer heat to speed the cure of the paint job. Protools*

*Fabricated booths need control of in-coming air, just like the professional models. Intake filter material like this is available in various sizes and configurations to fit any situation at very reasonable cost. Remember any fan you use in the booth needs to be rated "explosion proof." Dayton Reliable Air Filter*

across the back and you need no more hose than that. Other wise it's in your way and its causing extra loss in pressure.

We had another guy who was having constant fish eye problems with everything he painted. Well he forgot to look around. Three bays up, there was a clean-up shop. If the wind was blowing in the right direction all of that silicone the clean-up crew was using on the leather and vinyls would float right down to his shop and get into his intake filter and screw up his paint jobs. So you have to look around you to make sure there is nothing else in the room like WD 40 and Armor All and products containing high amounts of silicone oils.

## THE SPRAY BOOTH

Painters working in big shops probably already have a paint booth, maybe one of the newer down draft booths, those are great. But if you're painting at home or in a small shop you have to remember: the most important thing is air movement because if you're not moving any air you're not pulling the solvent out of the paint. If you're spraying in a dead air space it takes that much longer for the solvent to be pulled out of the paint film. You need air movement and a good exhaust fan that's filtering the air that's going outside so that you're not putting contaminates onto your neighbor's land or into the air. They have what they call arresting filters that grab the over-spray and catch it before it gets outside.

For setting up a paint booth, sheets of poly don't really work well, except for a single paint job. Once the plastic has paint on it, the dried paint will flake off and create dirt that contaminates the next paint job. A better idea is to build something with masonite panels. They even have these pre-made bathroom panels, it's like masonite with a coating on it. If you're going to make a spray booth at home in one of your stalls that stuff is not too expensive and it holds up real well. Anything you use is alright as long as you paint it first so it holds the dirt down and you can clean the walls, that's the main thing. And don't forget the old tricks like wetting the floor down before you do your painting.

*The air leaving the booth needs to be filtered as well, with arresting filters that eliminate most of the odor and paint mist.*

## Heat

To start with, I really don't like to see anybody paint in temperatures below 70 degrees. The problem with cooler temperatures is the way the solvents leave the paint film. When it goes below 70 degrees, even two or three degrees, you can read the differences in the paint. I know there are painters who paint in 60 degrees but my true belief is that you are never going to get quality in those kinds of temperatures because you have to wait so long between coats to get

*Typical fluorescent bulbs do not contain all the colors of the spectrum and do not accurately portray colors. These bulbs from the hardware store are just one one of the brands that will provide a true color of that new paint job.*

the solvents to leave, it's just not worth it.

Now how are you going to get some temperature in your spray booth? One of the best ways of course is a hot water heating boiler that's in a different part of the building, you can pump hot water into some small radiators or cast iron baseboard units. You could even use baseboard heating because there is no chance of the fumes contacting any open flame. There are people painting with log burning furnaces in their garages but that can be highly dangerous. Any open flame is dangerous, unless its highly elevated and that doesn't even help when you're painting because

the fumes seem to go everywhere. You have to understand those are a source of combustion because it is a flammable mist. Forced air can work but there are problems with hot spots and dust being blown around the room.

You really have to engineer your heating system properly. Of course you can buy a booth that has a heat source that actually heats the booth. That's ideal because then you have full control of the temperature when you're painting and they have a dry cycle that can actually bake the paint after a certain time. With the fan running you can gradually introduce heat and then you can fast-cure jobs to do more paint jobs during the day. And of course that's a more professional level not a hobby level.

## LIGHTING

Most everyone uses fluorescent lighting but the typical fluorescent light isn't a full-spectrum light. The full spectrum lights are available from companies like ParaLite and a number of other suppliers. If you use the regular cheap fluorescent bulbs from the hardware store the color in the booth isn't accurate so it's hard to judge the color of your paint job. A pure white light is necessary if you're trying to match colors. It's important to have the right lighting.

## SAFETY

You always need fire extinguishers, always put them by your exits. They have to be hung on the wall, they're not legal if they're sitting on the floor. You want them where it's easy to grab 'em. Familiarize yourself with their use so it's easy to just point it at the fire and pull the trigger if you ever do have a fire. They make powdered ones and they make the CO2 fire extinguishers. The Halon-style are the cleanest because there is no mess, but you can't use them in a closed space because they deplete the oxygen.

*The use of any catalyzed paints requires the use of a fresh-air hood to ensure you don't breath any of the paint fumes. The painter's suit protects you from the paint fumes as well, but it also keeps lint from your clothing out of the finished paint job. DeVilbiss*

Many communities require sprinkler heads in the spray booths. I have to do it but I cover my sprinkler heads with sandwich bags and rubber bands so they don't get contaminated and if it gets hot enough they are still going to go off but it keeps them protected in the booth. And some cities will make you put in a dry system, that is what I see most of the time in big professional booths. They have the huge container that mounts on the side of the booth and it puts out a dry powder if there is a fire.

## PROTECT YOUR LUNGS

Our basecoats are non-catalyzed, and when I'm using these in the booth I typically use only a TC-23 style of mask with the cartridges intended for use in a body shop environment. The trouble with these masks is the fact that they're not approved for use with catalyzed paints, and you have to be sure your beard or mustache isn't preventing the mask from sealing around your face.

When using today's catalyzed paints a regular TC-23 style face mask is not adequate. Having a hood that's supplying you with fresh air through a special filter is the ideal set up and they're not that costly.

The air-supplied respirator uses specially filtered air from your compressor, or from its own compressor, to supply pressurized breathable air for the air hood. Because the air is constantly flowing through the hood, there's very little chance for paint fumes to seep in where you're going to breath them.

You have to think about where the compressor is picking up the air for the mask. You don't want the small compressor feed-

*Fire extinguishers used in body shops and paint booths need to be classed at least A and B (common combustibles and flammable liquid).*

*This three-stage filter is what I use to convert air from the air compressor into breathable air. Left to right there's a 5 micron particulate filter, a 1 micron coalescing filter and a charcoal filter for odors and hydrocarbons.*

13

*This Painter Pro is made from silicone for maximum comfort and comes in three sizes for a good fit. Not approved for use with isocyanate paints. DeVilbiss*

*For painting isocyanate paints you need a fresh air hood, fed by specially filtered air supplied by a separate air hose. One of the nice things about these hoods is the cooling effect of the air when you're working in a hot spray booth. DeVilbiss*

ing the hood to draw in contaminated air or you've defeated the whole purpose of the air-supply hood.

And for spraying even non-catalyzed paints and primers in an area with poor air flow it's a good idea to use a full air-supply hood. Take the best care possible of your lungs – they are irreplaceable.

## A Painter's Suit

We have proven that by allowing T-shirts and straight clothes in the paint booth the amount lint and dirt in the final paint job is increased. A good painter's suit, such as the Shoot Suit out of Seattle, Washington is one of my favorites. It's not only cool to work in because the whole back of the suit breathes, but it prevents the lint on your clothes from finding their way into the paint job.

## Efficient Work Flow

Everybody's going to want to do this in their own way, but it's something to think about. It kind of becomes a personal thing how you want to have the work flow through the shop. It's difficult to do body work in the room where you are painting (we made some exceptions to that rule for this book because the lighting in the booth is so much better than it is in the shop and it made for better photography). Ideally

14

you want to separate the body work from the paint work but that may not be possible in a small shop.

Flowing the work and having your tools and equipment in a perimeter makes it easier and faster to get the work done. It's common sense stuff, your sand paper should be in a close proximity of all of you body work stuff so you are not traveling long distances or running around in circles trying to get things. When you have a big tool box you're not going to move that around so you want a little rolling tray set up so that you can put your tools and incidentals in it and have them close at hand.

## DEALING WITH FLAMMABLE AND TOXIC WASTE

You need to think about all the toxic and flammable chemicals in your shop. At my shop I like to keep everything in cabinets or containers. You may be required to install a flammable storage cabinet. Properly disposing of the used thinners and paint is critical. These materials have to be properly reclaimed or recycled. If you're working out of a small shop, you may be able to add your used chemicals to the waste of a big shop, where they have a service come and pick up the material. We use a distiller to reclaim the materials in the shop and get all our clean up material that way. What we can't distill goes off as hazardous waste. If the amount of hazardous waste you produce is small, you can usually take it to the approved waste facility in the county where you live.

*TC-23 type respirators like this come with replaceable filter cartridges. Most use a pre-filter to extend the life of the cartridge. Be sure cartridges are meant for a body shop environment - and keep them in some kind of sealed container (a coffee can works well) when not in use.*

# Chapter Two

# Modern Paint

## The Magic in the Can

**BEFORE THE PRIMER**

Before painting bare metal you need to make sure it's clean. Be certain that the product you use is specified as a final wash or a cleaning solvent. One of my favorites is a product called GON. You can also use thinners, acetone is another product that I use quite frequently. The most important thing is don't wet an area out larger than you can wipe off before it dries. Because if it dries before you get back to wipe it, it leaves a film. So in

*The House of Kolor line includes everything from final wash to the brightest kandys and pearls you've ever seen. We strive to create paints that give the flash and depth everyone is looking for without the work often associated with kandy and pearl paint jobs. Valspar*

other words a two by two foot area is about the largest I like to see wet out and then you need to come back immediately with a clean, dry cloth and dry it off.

There are times I don't use anything stronger than water. After color sanding for example, I use water because if the water doesn't go there it's telling you there's contamination at that point. I don't use chemicals when I'm color sanding and re-flowing an existing paint job, and you have to remember to keep bare skin off the paint job as you work because it transfers the oils. This rule is used from the time the job is started until the polishing, at that point the skin contact is no problem.

There is absolutely no reason to use a chemical wipe after a color sand unless someone has erroneously put some spray on there that might contain silicone such as Armor All or even WD 40 trying to lube a hinge or something like that. Armor All contains silicone that can contaminate the job and cause a tremendous amount of fish eye damage. Putting in the fish eye preventatives is one of the worst things you can do because then that job is going to require that additive each and every time. You're much better off using our KE 170 which is an encapsulated version of silicone which means you can use it to eliminate the fish eyes and not use it in succeeding coats.

*I like to use two clean rags when I wipe down the car before applying paint. One rag is wet with the product I'm using and the other is dry. The area I work isn't very big, I just wipe it on and wipe it off right away. The cleaner should never dry on the surface.*

*The substrate you're painting must be clean or the paint won't stick. These final-wash products include one that's solvent based (KC 10) and one water based (KC 20). Valspar*

## PRIMER

If a car has been completely chemically stripped or media blasted and you're down to the bare steel one of the most important things in my mind is an epoxy two-part catalyzed primer. I do not believe in metal etching compounds that you wipe on a car because we have seen delaminations caused by improper use of those compounds. They leave a film, and maybe they work fine with specific primers. Usually they do not work that well with epoxy primers.

When it comes to primer, we really feel that the epoxy primers are the most flexible and have the best adhesion. They out perform all other primers, that's why in the custom painting world they have been the preferred primer to use. You want a primer that has additives in it, the additives prevent plastic filler bleed through which has been a common problem in the past. The fact that it's catalyzed does not necessarily mean that it's going to prevent the plastic filler bleed through from the benzoil peroxides in the filler. And so this is a critical item at the start of your paint job. The paint job is only as good as the foundation and if the foundation is weak then what do you have? You have a job that won't live long-term.

Lacquer primers are proven to be porous, they are proven to have terrible adhesion to bare substrates. They're not a good thing because they can be moved by active solvent and that's what we use in our paints. We used to hear all these people crying about sand scratches swelling up in their paint job. What was happening was the lacquer primer was being wet out by the high quality solvents in the paint and the paint was sinking down into those 24 grit scratches in the metal or filler. Lacquer primers and lacquer putties can not be used for a quality long lasting paint job.

Catalyzed putties and body fillers are the best, but of course they also have to be properly mixed. The way that many painters and body men mix the mud is wrong. They mix air bubbles into it because they're churning it rather than flattening it out. I know that the plastic filler manufacturing companies don't recommend mixing on cardboard but if you do it quickly and if it's cardboard without printing on it, then it works OK. The box you get fenders or quarter panels delivered in can be cut into sixteen inch squares and kept under the bench. These make a perfect board because you use both sides and then you throw them away.

You can also get the plastic mixing boards but you have to keep them super clean. We had one guy that was having all kinds of problems with his body filler, we come to find out he's mixing his plastic filler on an irregular surface and that meant it wasn't uniformly mixed. All it takes is one section to be not properly catalyzed. It sounds simple but you know those mistakes are horrendous when the job is done and you've gone through all of that work

*Our new KP 2 CF is chromate free (thus the name), yet it remains a high-quality fast-build primer that will withstand hundreds of hours in the salt-spray test cabinet. Best of all, it sands very easily. Valspar*

and you end up with a bubble in the panel.

## DON'T FORGET SEALER

Yes, many painters like to omit the sealer, figuring that a good sanded primer is all they need. I always tell painters there are three things that a sealer does: 1. It prevents the penetration of the solvents into the primer. Now if you used a two-part primer that's not a real concern, but then again it does give you better color hold out by having used the sealer. 2. The second thing that a sealer does is create a bond between the properly sanded primer and the topcoat paint, that bond is critical. This is very much like using a bond coat when you're re-coating a clear. It creates that adhesive quality that makes the paint stick and you greatly reduce the chance of paint running. 3. Of course one of the most important things that a sealer does is make the vehicle all one color. Hopefully you've chosen a sealer that's very near to the basecoat color. That way it's easy to get good coverage with fewer coats. We are one of the few companies that makes a metallic sealer and that metallic sealer works great and not only that, it can be tinted to match varying shades of basecoats by using the KK concentrates, I do that quite frequently and we have an example of that in Chapter Four.

You have to carefully watch the time period after the application of sealer.

*The filler you use needs to be well mixed and applied to a surface it can stick to. You can't do a good paint job without doing good body work.*

*Our Ko-seal product is catalyzed for durability, and comes in three colors to better match the basecoat. Valspar*

If one of the available colors doesn't match the basecoat, you can also tint the sealer with any of our KK products. *Valspar*

The PBC products are part of the Shimrin line, known for easy application, fast dry times and great color. *Valspar*

Wait too long and the window of adhesion of succeeding coats closes causing delamination. To extend that time or for applying art over a sealer, apply one or two coats of SG 100, now the window is open for an additional one to four hours depending on the temperature and conditions in your booth.

Sealers have been considered important from the beginning of my painting career. I continue to use them today. To find me painting something without sealing, it just never happens.

## BASECOATS

For our base coats we have chosen to use a pure acrylic urethane resin and not catalyze it. How do we get away with this? We get away with this by using a proprietary co-polymer that makes the material behave like a lacquer. It does not have the chemical resistance of lacquer or urethane at it's early stages but when you top coat it with the catalyzed clear or a kandy it becomes as tough as it gets. The amazing thing about it is that three medium coats of the base puts on only 1/2 mil. It keeps the film thickness low, which is very important to me as a custom painter. I don't like to see my custom paint job exceed 15 mils even with multiple layers of art, kandys and clears.

In the old days many painters thought more coats meant a better paint job, well we learned very quickly in the lacquer era that those paint jobs didn't last more than a year or two and they shattered. More is not better. With the urethanes the amazing thing is you can do a quality paint job in the 10-mil range. And if there is art work, yes it might run to 12 and even as high as 15 mils but our coatings are designed for this mil thickness. The average paint job that you buy on a new car today is three to four mils. So it took some engineering to make these paint jobs hold up. And of course the beginning of any paint job is the foundation of two-part epoxy primer.

## KANDIES

One of the things that we pioneered is kandies with the same clarity and quality of color that we used to see in the old nitrocellulose paints. We originally did it with the acrylic lacquers and then in the early 80's we were able to achieve the same pure colors with our acrylic urethanes. So we have the high translucency and quality of color. We have designed these so that you can get the color depth and long lasting quality in just five to six coats of kandy. We do this by using extra milling time when we grind the pigments. When we mill some of these pigments it's not uncommon to go 100 hours in a ball mill or two-roll mill. It helps us to achieve that really good transparency. We spend the time that it takes to make them real transparent and that's very important to the painter because it all translates to ease of application. The more transparent and the more colorfast that these colors are the better they are.

Now don't cut your top-coat short based on your basecoat. If you're using the brightest and most reflective base color like silver or white pearl, its obvious that there's going to be more rebound of light. That the ultraviolet rays are going to rebound off the lighter more bright and reflective bases. In these cases you need to use the maximum number of kandy coats, which would be in the five to six coat range.

Now, this can also vary by your nozzle and needle size, your spray technique and air pressure. All of these things can change how much paint transfers to that surface. Of course the HVLP guns are extremely good at getting a 65% transfer efficiency. Some of the old guns would probably do half of that and so we really feel that the HVLP guns not only do a better job of applying the kandy coatings, but make sure you're getting the coating on the surface rather than up your exhaust stack and into the atmosphere. The newer guns atomize and control the spray pattern much better than the older technology.

## KANDY APPLICATION TECHNIQUES

One of the things that I pioneered is a certain type of pattern overlap. If you study a gun pattern, most of them are bowed in the middle. Which means that the very center of the pattern is the hot spot. If you use a 50% pattern overlap, one pass

*Each pass from the paint gun should overlap the last by the amount stated in the technical data sheet provided by the manufacturer for each product. For this basecoat I'm overlapping each pass by 50%.*

overlaps the last pass by one half or in the middle. That means that the hot spots are separated and that can lead to a stripe in the kandy job. By tightening that up and overlapping the first pass by 75% you reduce any chance of striping because the two hot spots are now in the center of the pattern. You do still have to be careful to hold the gun correctly though. What I call a parallel air cap is mandatory for proper pearl or kandy paint application.

*To get nice even coverage with kandy products I recommend a 75% overlap.*

We deal with this more in Chapter Three, but with kandy the gun technique is very very important. If you're holding the gun properly, and by that we mean paralleling the air cap, then you are much less likely to create a streak. We see painters working on the hoods of cars, they are not paralleling the air cap. They are drooping the gun and letting it drift, which is going to put a steak in the paint. Your gun handling has to be robotic. You also have to engineer the object for proper paint application.

## KANDY AND CLEAR

When a kandy job is completed I generally like to use the UC 35 clear because that is our pure acrylic clear and I'll put on two coats to preserve that job and give me enough room for color sanding. Then once it is color sanded and flow coated I'll switch over to the UFC 35 which is a polyester modified acrylic and it has more flexibility, higher gloss and is eas-

*Our kandy products can be used over any of our basecoats for an almost infinite number of colors and effects. Valspar*

ier to buff. Because it's an easier buffing clear it requires a little more cure time. I don't like to see a car buffed until 48 hours have passed.

The UC 35 is my build up clear because it's a pure acrylic and it gets hard very quickly. It doesn't have any rubbery tendencies from putting it on thick if you follow the dry times that are specified and let it get dry enough to the touch that it's not stringing-up and you're ready for the next coat. As far as spray techniques, when I re-flow the car I generally put a bond coat on, which is a coat put on very quickly with the gun held close with a slight amount of extra reduction, (25-50% of extra reducer on those flow coats) and then follow up with two more solid wet coats. You know I figure you might sand off one-half mil when you do the color sanding with the 500 before you re-flow the paint. Then when you sand with 1200 you take off very little paint, you're just knocking down the lint and the minor orange peel from the gun. Because of that extra reducer if the gun is held close and the clear is put on super wet the amount of orange peel that is left is negligible. I mean they look like a good old lacquer job, except for the extra gloss and the maintenance-free nature of these new urethanes.

## NEW PRODUCTS

Probably the most exciting of all the new products that are either available now or coming to market are the

*Our catalyzed UC 35 clear is quick drying and good for burying art work. It's not always the best product for the final clear however. Valspar*

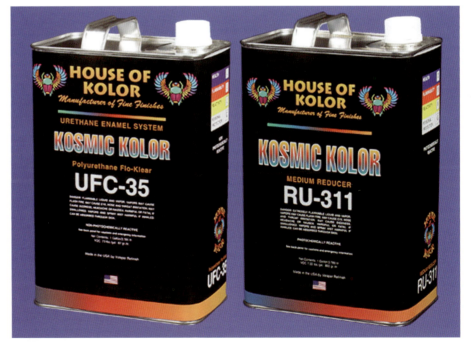

*Any of our reducers can be used with our UFC clear (also catalyzed). This product makes a good final clear because it buffs easily and stays flexible. Valspar*

new Kameleon II dry powders. I know many people freak out when they look at the price. You get two ounces for about three hundred dollars, and that seems like a lot of money. But our first Kameleon, the liquid material that we came out with, is about two hundred and fifty dollars for a pint and that makes up to a quart of sprayable material. With the new dry material you get two ounces in the container and when you mix it with SG 100 it makes 4 gallons of ready-to-spray material. So it's a great buy for a color-change product, it works for ghosting flames and so many different things.

The best thing is it does not bronze when it goes through its changes. For example, the blue-to-green, if you hold it at eye level it's a beautiful true blue. As you move it down towards your belt buckle it starts to go turquoise and when you reach your belt buckle it's a beautiful green. There is no bronzing taking place in any of those transitions.

There are four colors available now and four new ones in the works. As soon as those pass Florida testing they will be available to our customers. The other thing that I am excited about is the new MBC basecoats (metallic base coat); they are really exciting because they have a medium flake look without the work. They go on like a regular base coat and you apply the kandy right over them and they have such a flash and sparkle in the sun it completely dazzles you when you see how easy it was to achieve. Yes, they are a little expensive, I believe as of this writing they are about a hundred and seventeen dollars a quart, but it's amazing the amount of work they save and how beautiful they are under kandies.

We make one that's called pale gold, MBC 01, another that's called platinum, MBC 02 and a third named black diamond, MBC 03. They all impart different looks in the kandy colors. In fact the Camaro painting sequence in this book is done just that way, we used all three bases with one kandy color sprayed over the top and you can see the radical change that takes place on that car. This paint is magnificent stuff to work with and again it's a low-solids paint. It doesn't have the build up that you would normally associate with something with this much glitter.

Some of the other things that we are slowly starting to get out now are these new brilliant pearlescent powders and they are going to be available in about 15 colors when we get them all tested. Right now we have the whitest white that's been available since the old lead carbonate pearls. This has a tremendous brilliance to it and the same grain size as our existing white pearl. but it has so much more brilliance and flash to it you would swear that it's four grain sizes larger. It's just the way that these pearls are made that they impart this extra bit of brilliance. So be

*Non-catalyzed and reduced with any of our reducers, the MBC series of paints use a new flake material that's just super bright and makes for some brilliant paint jobs.*

watching for what we're now calling the X pearls (the final brand name might be different). They are an amazing product and will dominate the pearl world in the future.

There are also a couple of new kandy colors and some new basecoats that are being tested right now, but we don't know yet if they are going to survive Florida's testing. We use a carbon-arc machine that emulates the sun, that's our first test point. If they pass that test they go to Florida where we do a lot of sub tropical testing. This is done with the painted object in a black box which really draws the heat along with the sun's rays and that seems to be the place that breaks a paint down the quickest. We are not going to put anything out there that's going to fail.

There's also a new yellow neon pigment being developed right now that's designed to stand up to the sun like a regular automotive pigment, to survive the black-box test. Our other neons are made with very fragile dyes and do not have long life, which everyone understands. Typically they're used for race cars and that kind of thing. It will be exciting to have a neon that can live in the sun.

*These new Kameleon Pearls should be mixed with SG 100. They are less expensive (per volume) than our earlier product and give a cleaner color change. Valspar*

*The new Kameleons are great for art work, graphics and flames - as is illustrated by this motorcycle tank from Chapter Six.*

# Chapter Three

# Spray Guns

## Guns and Pattern Control

### WHAT IS HVLP

Spray guns have gone through a tremendous change just in the last two or three years. The new guns don't just get a higher percentage of the paint onto whatever you're painting, they atomize the paint much better as well, which makes for better kandy and pearl application.

People think HVLP – High Volume Low Pressure – means these guns put out a high volume of paint. Yes, they do have great transfer effi-

*The new spray guns do a great job of atomizing the paint at the nozzle. Which makes for better, more consistent paint application and a smoother finish. DeVilbiss*

ciency but the volume being referred to is the much larger volume of air required to operate the gun. These new spray guns need more air than the earlier guns. In fact most HVLP guns are in the 16,17,18,19 or more CFM (cubic feet per minute) range and that's pretty high considering some of the older guns required only 10,12, or 14 CFM. The low pressure part of the definition refers to the pressure at the air cap, which must be ten pounds or less.

These newer guns need a greater volume of air so that means the old 5/16 inch hoses and fittings and couplers no longer work. Now we need a 3/8 inch hose, one specifically designed for painting so it doesn't fragment on the inside. When you buy a hose, don't buy a cheap hose for the spray booth. I buy the good hoses and when they get

*Known for good atomization and a transfer efficiency greater than 65%, the Plus gun also puts out 15% more paint volume than similar guns. Comes with EZ Liner disposable paint liners. DeVilbiss*

tired in the booth I retire them into the shop and put a new hose in the booth. Generally you should do that once or twice a year depending on how much use the hose receives. We need the much larger fittings too (note the photos), they are almost double the size compared to the old ones.

Though we mentioned this in Chapter One, it bears repeating. If you have a 5/16 inch hose 40 feet long with the 5/16 inch fittings the pressure at your gun can be reduced by up to 10 -15 or more pounds compared to what you have at the regulator. With a 3/8 inch hose and the larger fittings we have found that the pressure drop is negligible. I do not believe in cheater valves, you will never see me with a cheater valve on a gun.

You need a working regulator in the booth that's proper and accurate. In order to know what

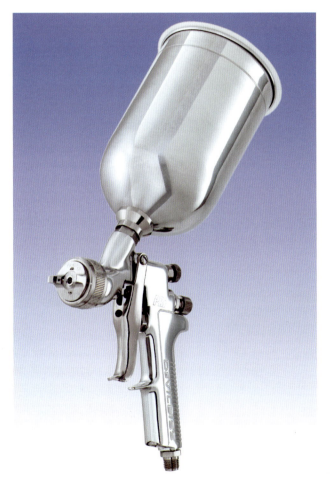

*HVLP PRi gun comes with the specific air cap designed to atomize and move the low VOC, high-solids, primer materials. DeVilbiss*

*A full range of hose ends and disconnects are available with larger inside diameters to minimize pressure drop in your air hose. DeVilbiss*

the pressure drop is, put a pressure gauge at the end of the hose that supplies the gun. Now you know what is going on in your spray booth.

Some of the new guns aren't actually HVLP. DeVilbiss claims their new "Plus" gun is the best spray gun they have ever made. They proved to the Air Resource Board in Southern California that 10 PSI at the air cap meant nothing. What the Air Resource Board wanted was a 65% fluid transfer ratio and DeVilbiss proved to them that they can do that while putting more pressure at the air cap. The newer paints are all higher solids and the additional pressure at the air cap helps the gun atomize the higher-solids paint.

SADA has also developed a gun that uses higher pressure at the air cap while still providing a 65% transfer efficiency. These are two guns that I know of, there are others as well, that are atomizing the new high solids products and that are doing a great job of it. I am working with these companies because this is going to continue, the government intervention in the industry and changes to the various products. Water-borne base coats are one of the things that are in the works though we don't know how many years off those are. They asked us to work on this and we already are.

*High quality air tool hose (in red) is available in bulk or with ends already attached (5/16 and 3/8 inch ID). Fluid transfer hose (black) is resistant to most water-based and solvent-based paints and resins used in the body shop environment. DeVilbiss*

I should mention one other gun, the Iwata. It does great atomization of the paint but it's not comfortable for everyone because the handle is small. If you are a person with small hands though, or for a women who is going into custom painting, you may want to take a look at this particular gun because of the size and quality.

## HOW MANY GUNS?

People sometimes ask me how many guns they need in a small shop. I really like to see a dedicated clear and kandy gun. The same gun you kandy with can also be used to apply clear, with a fluid tip change. But anything you use to shoot metallic or pearl should be a dedicated metallic/pearl gun. Because it's a sad case scenario when grit or dirt or a piece of metallic gets out in your clear coat over a kandy job and ruins the look of it and that's not uncommon. Even here in our shop where we have 50 or 60 guns at our disposal I have made that mistake by picking up the wrong spray gun.

So unless you're very thorough and completely break the gun down after each use and clean it, it's a good idea to have a dedicated gun for metallic and pearls.

Also, I really feel that a cheaper gun dedicated to primer is a good idea. Particularly these high solid primers. You need a 1.8 to 2.2mm nozzle-needle combination to move those higher-

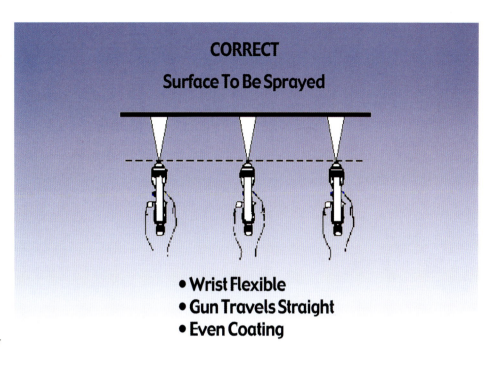

**CORRECT**
**Surface To Be Sprayed**

- **Wrist Flexible**
- **Gun Travels Straight**
- **Even Coating**

*The air cap must stay parallel to the surface...*

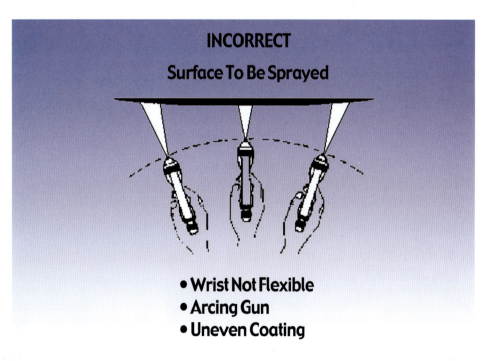

**INCORRECT**
**Surface To Be Sprayed**

- **Wrist Not Flexible**
- **Arcing Gun**
- **Uneven Coating**

*...or the paint application will not be uniform. You need straight line, robotic thinking. DeVilbiss*

# Adjust the Pattern

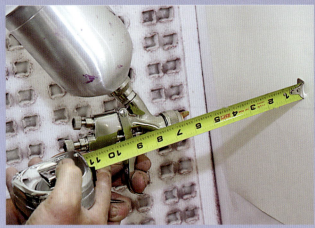

We start with the gun six inches from the wall, our goal is a pattern six inches wide.

...with the gun six inches from the wall I try again.

Our first pattern is too wide and uneven.

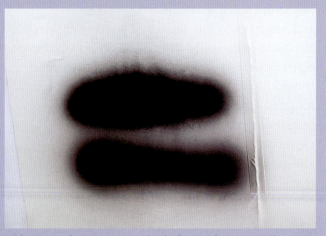

The second pattern is a little better but it's still uneven.

So we clean the tip of the fluid nozzle and the air cap with solvent and a soft-bristle brush...

After installing a new air cap I try one more time but it's still too wide and a bit uneven.

# Adjust the Pattern

## PATTERN CONTROL

It's important to check your pattern each time you paint. You only have control of the pattern within about six or seven inches from the air cap. Past that the fine atomized mist created by the air horns, starts to coalesce into globs of paint. Orange peel and blotching are the result of poor gun control. I generally set the gun up for either a six inch pattern six inches from the gun, or a four inch pattern four inches from the gun. I use the six inch pattern on cars and bigger objects, and the smaller pattern on motorcycles and smaller parts. For this demonstration I've loaded the spray gun up with black primer, something that will show up on the white paper.

## THE MATERIAL CONTROL ADJUSTMENT

I like to leave the upper adjustment, air to the horns, wide open and adjust the pattern with the material knob. The first series of patterns shows the importance of keeping your guns clean. Even with a new air cap I can't get a nice even pattern so I give up and start over with a different spray gun.

## SEQUENCE NUMBER TWO

The second sequence goes better, this is more typical of the adjustments you would go through before starting a paint job. Basically, the pattern starts out too wide and I use the material knob to constrict the pattern until it's four inches wide.

## PATTERN OVERLAP

The last photos in this sequence help to explain exactly what I mean when I say you need to have 50 or 75% pattern overlap when painting. Because you can't be sloppy. Not in the size of the pattern, the gun-to-subject distance or the overlap from one pass to the next.

Note: Throughout this book our 6-photo sequences like the one on page 30 and 32 start at the top left, read down to the bottom, then across to the top right and then down again.

*Gun 2: I like to start with the fan (top) adjustment wide open and the material knob about 2 turns out.*

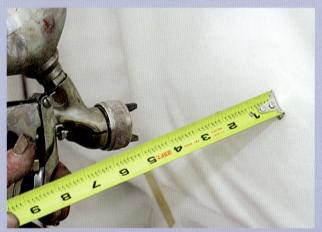

*This time we start with the gun 4 inches from the wall.*

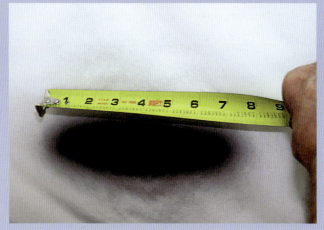

*Our goal is a pattern 4 inches wide, and we're close.*

# Adjust the Pattern

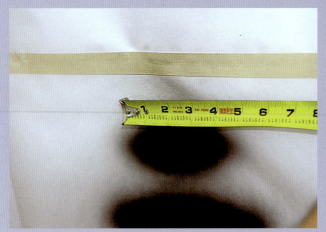

*I screw the material knob in further, now I get a nice pattern just over 4 inches wide.*

*For making horizontal patterns the horns need to be turned "up and down," don't forget...*

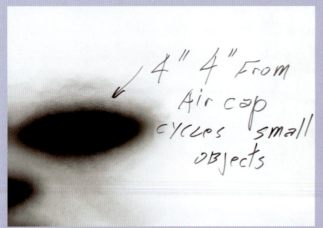

4" 4" From
Air cap
cycles small
objects

*I recommend a 4 inch pattern for small objects...*

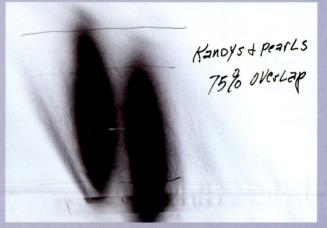

Kandys & Pearls
75% Overlap

*...to turn them back to their normal horizontal position for a standard vertical pattern.*

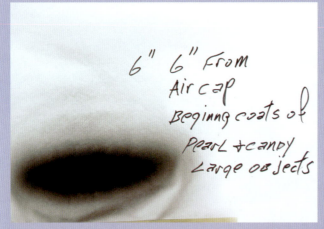

6" 6" From
Air cap
Beginng coats of
pearl & candy
large objects

*...and a 6 inch pattern for automobiles and larger objects.*

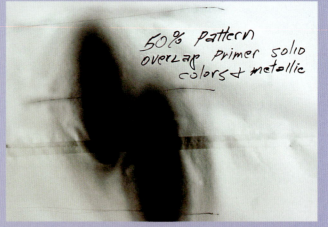

50% Pattern
overlap primer solid
colors & metallic

*These 2 demos illustrate the amount of overlap you need with kandies/pearls, and everything else.*

the Sharpe Platinum) is designed so that when you bring in the material knob you also reduce the pattern size. You need to know what a good working pattern is and how to achieve that pattern. This is generally based on the size of the object you're painting, note the pattern illustrations in this chapter.

My start up working pattern on a kandy job on motor cycles is a four inch pattern four inches from the end of the air cap and I

*On a typical spray gun the upper knob controls the amount of air to the horns. Normally I leave this control wide open.*

solid primers through the gun. Again, with catalyzed primers and spray filler always remove the fluid tip and clean thoroughly after each use. This is a must do item.

## GUN USE AND ADJUSTMENTS

The main thing to watch for when using a spray gun is the air pressure. That air pressure needs to be the pressure specified by the particular gun manufacturer. And make sure that you are actually achieving that gun pressure at the end of the spray hose (we talked earlier about pressure drop). One thing I like about the Geo gun is that it has a gauge tapped into the fitting at the base of the handle. SADA and Sharpe also have a pressure gauges built into the handle that tell you the pressure at the gun. Those are the only three guns I know of that have that feature. Other than that it's up to you, the professional, to put that gauge on and make sure that you are getting the pressure that the gun is specified to be using based on how many feet of hose that you have in the booth.

When I adjust a gun I like to start with the fan control wide open and the material knob about two turns out. Every paint gun on the market that I have worked with (with the exception of

*A few guns, like this Geo, have a gauge built into the handle so you always know exactly how much air you have at the gun.*

*I you look closely at this Sharpe gun, you can see a "tire gauge" type of pressure gauge built into the handle.*

use a tape measure to make sure I'm in that range. I don't guess. On an automobile I like a six inch pattern six inches from the gun as a start up pattern. With kandies I prefer a 75% pattern overlap, with a six inch pattern it's about a 1-1/2 inch increment each time. You have to graph out your object before the spraying begins and then use invisible straight lines as you spray. As we talk about repeatedly in the book, don't converge your passes to fit the sheet metal, use invisible straight lines with a band pass to tie it all together.

## APPLICATION TECHNIQUES

I call it paralleling the air cap. That is, the air cap must be parallel to the surface you're trying to paint. Make sure that you don't have lazy-painters-syndrome where you droop the gun down and it's not parallel to the surface. Obviously in that case the top of the pattern is going to have a streak, or if the panel sways away at the bottom part of the car if you're not aiming at that you are going to streak from the top of the pattern rather than from the bottom of the pattern. I tell painters, 'I want you to behave like a robot. You know what you have to do, you know what your approximate gun distance is, you've adjusted the gun so that you know what the pattern size is.'

Many painters fail when trying to do a kandy paint job by using a full trigger pull. You can't use a full trigger pull because you're letting the paint run wild. Then to compensate you start to move the gun away from the surface, which increases the platelet droplet size to almost a drop. Bigger droplet size creates that stucco effect that can also cause excessive orange peel.

The finest atomization occurs where the gun breaks up the paint at the air cap.

*You have to know how much pressure you have at the gun, either with a gauge built in to the gun, or one added on between the handle and the hose. DeVilbiss*

As those little particles of spray paint move farther away from the gun they collide and grow. That's why we don't like to see a painter work further than six to seven inches from the surface. That's the maximum distance we recommend.

The painter needs to get tuned in to adjusting the gun. He or she also has to learn to work close and use a tight pattern overlap with kandies and pearls. And admittedly it takes time. You have to learn to walk the length of an object. If you're painting a car you can't stop at a fender and pick it up at the end of the door, because every time the spray gun stops and starts the millage increases, its an act of physics beyond the painter's control, it's something that just happens. A kandy job done that way will show the dark stripe around the door because of the stopping and starting. Yes it takes a little practice to learn to walk and take those short steps and hold that gun properly like the robot that you are and wear a painter's suit, but it's all worth it if you want to become a truly good custom painter.

Hose control is a very important consideration when you walk. Don't allow kinks to develop in the hose, always keep the hose behind you so it doesn't trip you up. How fast you walk determines the gun speed. Concentrate on the paint hitting the surface.

*We've said it before, it's essential that the air cap be kept parallel to the surface you're painting.*

*Sometimes I put the hose over my shoulder, that way I always know exactly where it is. And I never have more hose in the booth than I need.*

# Chapter Four

# Tri-Color Camaro

## It's All About The Basecoats

Our project for this chapter is a complete paint job on a 1977 Camaro. The body is already stripped completely. The metal body panels were stripped chemically, the big aluminum bumpers are off the car, we will dress with the DA, prime with our KP 2 CF and then paint in body color. You could also sand blast the bumpers before applying the primer.

For chemical stripping the best thing to use is coarse steel wool, once the stripper has done its

*This is the start of the project. A 1977 Camaro that's been chemically stripped. By working on the bare metal we don't have to worry about working over old filler or whether our paint will react with materials already on the car.*

job. Putty knives leave deep gouges in the metal. And you need to have a box or bag to catch all the material so it doesn't collect on the floor.

## More Prep Work

There are holes in the body where old body work was done on the left front fender and where the big Camaro emblems were screwed to the body. All those holes will be countersunk and then brazed shut. We countersink them a little so the weld can't drop into the body. The little nibs along the bottom of the door that hold on trim, those will be ground off because I don't like that big molding there anyway.

Before we're done we will re-fit the doors, we also have to pull the glass and DA the edges of all the openings. At the front fender there's an old body repair, someone drilled holes and then pulled the dent out, and didn't fill the holes. If you drill holes you need to weld them shut after pulling the dent. You could also use a stud gun, and that way you wouldn't have any holes at all.

I like to have fresh metal around those holes before I come back and weld them. And as long as I'm working in this area I'm going to put on a glove and check for dents. Then I can do a little grinding around any of those little dents, usually with 24 grit, so the filler has something to get a hold of. The glove is so important, you need to have your fingers together as you move over the area, not apart, and move quickly across the panel. You can really find the dents this way. I see guys doing this with their fingers spread out and that's the wrong way. And of course things will change a little after the areas are welded, due to the heat, so I'm going to go over the panel with the glove again after all the welding is finished.

We are using special wire-feed welding equipment that's setup for welding light-weight metal. After welding all the holes shut I go over the panels again with the grinder and knock off the extra metal with a 24 grit pad on the grinder. Then I want to run the glove over the area and feel for any low spots. Those need to be touched with the grinder so the mud has something to hang onto. If there's a low spot you have to get the grinding

*The bumpers are made from aluminum. I will scuff them with a DA before painting.*

*I like to use a tapered bit to countersink the holes in the body. That way the brazed or welded plug can't drop into the body.*

*There are some small holes in the front fender, part of an old dent repair. I like to scuff the area before welding the holes shut.*

Note: Our 6-panel pages are constructed in columns - they start on the top left, read down to the bottom, then across to the top right and down again.

I like to check the panel for high and low spots as early as possible, and it's much easier to feel those spots with a glove on your hand.

I use the wire-feed welder, set up to weld sheet metal with lighter wire, to weld shut all the small holes in the body.

After welding the holes shut I knock down the welds with a small grinder and 24 grit pad.

It's important to check the area after each weld and grind session.

A hammer and spoon is a good way to knock down a high spot without creating a series of small dents with the hammer.

Then it's time for another check. An experienced hand can be the best tool you have.

pad down into the bottom of the low spot. This has to do with adhesion, we want to make sure we have everything ground where we're going to have any mud.

Now that I have all the high and low spots identified, any that are exceptionally high need to be knocked down and there are two ways to deal with them, either a spoon or a pick. I like the spoon because it transfers the force of the blow to a larger area, you're not just making a series of dents in the metal.

## MIX THE FILLER

It's important to knead the hardener before use. The shelf life is about nine months, you can extend that by keeping it in the refrigerator. The manufacturers don't like it when you use cardboard for mixing the mud. Actually, you can use it if there's no printing on the cardboard and you don't leave the mud on for very long, it will absorb the resin in the mud if left on the cardboard too long. You can also use the plastic palette to do the mixing.

The filler and hardener must be thoroughly mixed, I like to go through it with a light stoke, then a medium stroke and then a hard stroke. I change the angle of the squeegee too as I'm working. Then I take everything off the plastic paddle and start over again with the three different strokes. You want uniformity in the blended product. If the filler and hardener are not mixed well the mud stays soft and creates a bubble later.

With the Gold Rage filler product the more hardener there is in the mix the darker the product becomes. In fact they provide a color chart that you can use as a guide. You will see streaks when it's not well mixed. I tell people to take the time to read the manufacturer's instructions.

You need to clean the palette right, with a horse-hair parts-cleaning brush and acetone and some old rags. I wipe off the squeegee first, then the mixing board. This way I don't have to worry about contaminant's from the last batch affecting the new batch.

## APPLICATION AND SANDING

If you're lucky you can do it in one. On the door there are low spots all the way across so I'm

*After mixing the filler thoroughly I start the application on the left front fender*

*By spending time in the application - applying only as much mud as is needed - you save time sanding and finishing later.*

*I pull the mud all the way across the door for a nice smooth application.*

39

It takes two applications to get one smooth coat of filler across the center of the door.

The mud hog equipped with a 40 grit pad is a great tool for shaping the mud early in the process.

The lower part of the door and rocker panel require their own application.

After going over all the filled areas with the mud hog I like to to go over them again with a power stick (also dust free) equipped with 36 grit paper.

We are using a dust-free system from Hutchens to sand the car as a means of minimizing the air-borne dust in the shop.

I like to check my progress often. The glove helps me identify high and low spots and I don't transfer oils from my hand to the body.

going to go back and grind all the way across the door before coming back with the mud.

I like to pull the mud all the way across the door if possible. It takes two applications to get the left side covered with one good coat of filler. Before it's completely hard I take a knife and trim off excess filler in areas where I know I don't want it.

We are sanding this with a dust-free system. When you're using a dust-free tool like this mud hog, you have to be careful in the way you put on the paper.

When you check for high and low spots it's important to wear a glove. This way as I check the body work and the progress with my hand I don't transfer any of the oils from my skin to the metal.

The mud talks to you, look at the low spot on the lower section of the left front fender, that dark spot says the mud hog didn't touch it and the reason is because that area's low. I'm using 36 grit on the power stick and 40 grit on the dust-free mud hog.

After going over the entire side of the car with a mud hog we go over it again with the power stick, also part of this dust-free system. Now I want to go over the whole side with a sanding block. I want this to go fast and have 36 grit paper on the block.

The hand blocking shows us more low spots so I think we're going to come back and do a skin coat over the area. To make sure the mud sticks to all the metal surfaces I'm going to go over the whole door skin with a DA and 80 grit pad. In fact we could have done this before we started with the filler work. You need to blow the car off with compressed air and a clean rag before applying any more filler.

## Second Application of Mud

If you look at the pictures (page 42) you can see I'm not putting this on very thick. The idea is to put this on as nice as you know how. I carefully add the second application all the way along the car, mixing only a relatively small amount each time.

*The mud talks to you, dark areas were never sanded because they're low.*

*Before doing another application I go over the filler with a long sanding block equipped with 36 grit paper.*

*Because of the low spots we need to skim coat the whole door, but before I do it's necessary to go over the entire door with a DA and 80 grit.*

After blowing off the car I start with the second coat of filler material, trying not to put on any more than necessary.

Before applying the spray filler it's important to blow all the loose dust off the body.

The sequence here is pretty much the same as what I did after the first application. Except that I go from the mud hog with 40 grit...

The gun we're using is a gravity-feed HVLP from DeVilbiss, for moving the heavier spray-filler material we need the 2.0mm tip seen on the right.

...straight to the hand block with 36 grit.

No matter what you're spraying, it's a good idea to do a test pattern.

Then I come in with a big mud hog and 40 grit paper to knock it down close and then I pretty much follow the same sequence I did with the first application of mud. Going across the left side with the mud hog you can see that we've filled the low spots that were left after the first application. Then I switch to the hand block with 36 grit. The blocking is very important. To get perfection you still have to work by hand. Now I go over the car one more time with a block and 80 grit paper to knock down the high spots from the 36 grit.

## SPRAY PUTTY

At this point we've gone over the whole car and done all the basic body work with 40 and 36 grit. I like to see the mud left at 40 or 36 and then take the tops off any remaining high spots with 80 grit. When it's all done with 80 it's harder for the primer to bridge the area between the metal and the body work. That's why I don't like to see people over-finish the body work. Let the primer be the bridge between the body work and substrate.

When a car is chemically stripped like this one it's important to sand all the metal, not just the areas near where the body work was done, because the stripping chemical leaves the metal in a condition that affects the adhesion of the filler. Whether its fiberglass or steel, I like an 80 grit etch so you know the primer will stick. And I like to use an orbital sander, like a DA, not a grinder because the grinder will leave swirl marks.

Now I mask off the windows. Big pieces of cardboard can be used for this and taped at the edges if the glass is removed. Before we go any farther I need to blow off the car with high pressure air. The next step is to wash it with KC 20.

This new spray body filler puts on 2 mils per coat, that's a lot. It's like taking a plastic body filler and reducing it so you can spray it. You can't paint over the spray filler because it will suck up the paint, you must use primer first. The primer we're using here is KP-2 CFA and KP-2 CFB, both products are chromate free.

We need a 2.0 or 1.8mm tip for the paint gun in order to shoot the spray filler. We need the big-

*The spray filler needs to be applied quickly after mixing. These fillers are available from DeBeer and Fibre Glass-Evercoat.*

*Like any paint material, the spray filler should be applied following straight line painting techniques.*

*Once it's applied, the spray filler looks like like any other primer coat.*

The sand paper won't be truly flat on the sanding block unless you get off all the old adhesive left behind.

It only takes a minute for the guide coat to dry, then I start block sanding (with the rods in place) using 80 grit paper on the block.

These block sanders from Adjustable Flexibility Sanders are great. They can be used with or without the rods to work in almost any situation.

We call it a guide coat because the remaining paint guides you to the low spots...

Back to the body work. Application of a guide coat is next - in this case I used modified dark primer.

...which we fill with catalyzed spot putty.

ger tip to move this heavier material. The gun is a gravity-feed DeVilbiss, HVLP "PRi" series gun (the part number is: Pri-601G-14). Also note photos of the two hose inlet fittings (page 8), how much larger the I.D. is on the one than the other. For HVLP you need a high volume of air and that includes the hose, which should be 3/8 I.D., and the bigger fittings.

The spray filler uses methyl ethyl ketone hardener, it is not an isocyanate product like the catalyzed paint. After adding the hardener and stirring it with the filler, without shaking, I spray the filler quickly. This material sets up so fast you don't have much time after you've added the hardener. We mask at this point, out of sequence because actually we should have been done this before the spray-filler was mixed.

The spray filler is sprayed just like paint or primer. I start by checking the pattern coming out of the gun on a piece of paper I have taped to the wall of the spray booth (page 42). Then I start at the right front corner and work my way around the car, always spraying in a straight line, with 50% overlap between each pass. I have the gun set at 40 psi at the wall and 36 at the gun. You can put a second coat of the spray-filler on immediately after you apply the first, it sets up quick.

## GUIDE COAT/SANDING BLOCKS

Next we guide coat all the areas where we applied spray filler yesterday. There is a product from Tempo that comes in an aerosol can, but in this case I over thinned number seventy dark gray primer and I'm using that as a guide coat.

OK, now we set up our blocks. First I like to razor the pads (note the photo pg 44) to be sure they're clean before I put down the new paper. Sometimes when you pull the old paper it leaves some residue behind, which happened here. The razor blade is a good way to make sure none of that residue remains. The blocks themselves are pretty interesting. I like these flexible pads because without the rods they will conform to the shape of a fender, if I put one rod in it's still a little flexible and when I want complete rigidity I just put all three rods in.

*The sanding block equipped with 80 grit will ensure the puttied area is level with the rest of the trunk.*

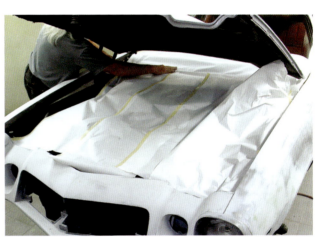

*Before the final primer I finish taping off the car, including areas under the hood. This also traps dust that might become airborne during painting.*

*It's important to wipe off the car with an appropriate final wash (not tar/wax and grease remover) before applying the final primer.*

*Wiping off the car is a multi-step process. The final stage is what I call 'air and tack.'*

*You can't be sloppy here just because it's primer. This is the practice session for the base and kandy paint to follow.*

*Note how I follow a straight line each time, with 50% overlap between each coat.*

I also like the orbital blocker made by National Detroit. It's great for getting down low, those areas are so hard to get down to when the car's not on a hoist. I tell custom painters 'whenever you can use a tool to get close, do it. It saves you so much time.'

I use an orbital power blocker and a large eight inch DA for doing finesse work on the flat areas, it's great on big flat areas. When it comes to the body work there are some other tools I like to use, these include the three inch, five inch and six inch orbital sanders and straight line sanders that use 16-5/8X2-3/4 paper. These are all non-vacuum sanders from Atcoa.

Sometimes when you're working on the second or third coat of filler, it's a good idea to start sanding before the new application is hard. That way you can work on the new material without getting into the old. People make the mistake of waiting for the second coat to dry and then when they sand they get into the first coat as well. That's when you start to chase yourself around. Once we hit bare metal, that's as far as we can go. And the dark areas are guide coat that we didn't sand off, those are the remaining low areas.

We use glazing putty to fill those small areas. What I'm using on the Camaro is catalyzed glazing putty. This is a fine filler and it's very fast. This material sets up so quick that you run to the car once it's mixed. If you are ready to paint a car you can do a little spot right before you paint. You don't have five minutes after you mix it. The idea is to put it on thin and neat so you don't have to do a lot of sanding. I'm using 80 grit here, both for sanding the spray filler and the spot putty. We're going to do some work on that quarter too, the left rear.

I've gone over the whole body with 80 grit, in fact I found a few more small dents in the roof which I fixed. The trim is out of the front and rear glass. For cleaning glass I use a damp rag with a little Acetone on it, which does a great job of cleaning the glass and getting rid of over-spray.

The primer we're using here is, KP-2 CFA and KP-2 CFB, Kwikure epoxy primer surfacer. The CF in these products stands for Chromate free.

## TAPING

I like to tape the key in place in the trunk so I'm sure I can open that. Sometimes the tape won't stick to the rubbers at the door and the trunk. In those cases AP 01 adhesion promoter can be used, just a light mist coat, to help the tape stick to the rubber. In this case we don't have any trouble, the tape sticks pretty good.

Now I have to blow off the car with compressed air before I do any more taping. Then I start under the hood (page 45). Some people use poly but I'm just going to use paper for this. I like to cover the entire engine, then I remove the door glass and install the cardboard in the doors. And we're ready to mix the primer.

For wiping the car down I like to use two rags that I've folded neatly. I put final wash on one of the rags and go over the car with that one first and then again with a second, dry, rag, working one two by two foot area at a time.

## PRIMER

The primer, both parts, need to be shaken or stirred thoroughly before being mixed together, then shaken or stirred thoroughly again after mixing. Once it's mixed it has a two to four hour shelf life.

I always use a tack rag from Crystal, it's the biggest company out there. It's important to take the tack rag out of the package and open it up 20 minutes before you use it. Then once it has aired you want to bundle it up in a loose ball. I call it air and tack, going over the entire car with the tack rag, while at the same time I'm blowing it off with the air gun.

For spraying the primer I use a gravity feed HVLP primer gun from DeVilbiss with a 1.8mm tip, running at 40 psi at the regulator. You should always be just as careful with the primer as you are with the topcoats. Applying primer is a good opportunity to practice your patterns for the kandy job. I'm careful with my gun distance and I lay it all out and shoot it with straight lines, using a straight-line pattern with 50% overlap. In total I'm going to put three coats of primer on this car with an extra two coats on the areas where we have body work. Once sprayed, the primer should

*After allowing the primer to cure and applying another light guide coat, I start block sanding in an X-pattern, using 400 grit paper.*

*These small, round, flexible sanding blocks are perfect for fender lips and other concave areas.*

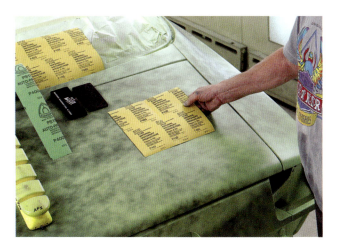

*The big sheets of 3M paper have to be cut to fit the small flexible sanding blocks.*

There are various ways to cut the big sheets of sandpaper. First I cut the paper in thirds...

The design I have in mind for this car will be done using three different base colors, all covered with the same kandy topcoat.

...then I wrap it around the block as shown.

After finding the center of the car I begin laying out the top stripe by eye using conventional masking tape.

These small blocks fit really nicely into the palm of your hand.

Right or wrong on these layouts is often just a matter of what you like. Don't be afraid to pull the tape and start over on a shape or design.

set up for 24 hours at 70 degrees. Otherwise you get seeding in the sandpaper from the partially cured primer.

## ANOTHER GUIDE COAT

I do a guide coat over the whole car at this point. And then it's time to block sand the whole thing. I think I've found all the areas that need body work but this will tell us for sure. We are block sanding with 400 grit wet, the strips I can put on the block, the 3M sheets I can cut and use in my hand.

There are various ways to fold the paper so you can use it in any direction without having it ball up in your hand. When we find a low area, that's where I concentrate.

For those rounded areas you can use one of these round sanding blocks, they're flexible too. The Dura-Block with its round shape is great for areas like the concave area on the top of the quarter where the regular sanding block won't work.

Now the body is completely primered. We are doing the final tape out prior to application of the base coat. After taping I like to wipe the car down and blow it off with compressed air.

Note: I did a little more dent repair just before applying the sealer and basecoats, and used fast cure primer, which has a slightly different color.

## THE LAYOUT

I tell people, 'find center first, then determine the shape of stripe on one side, by eye, measure that and duplicate it on the other hood.' We are using three different basecoats to create the design on this car. Even though this is a later Camaro, I want to do a Yenko type stripe on the car.

First I determine a shape I like. Then I mask that off with a 1/4 inch piece of regular masking tape, on the inside, then I run the 1/4 inch plastic tape that butts up against the 1/4 inch masking tape. The last thing I do is pull the guide tape, leaving the plastic tape. When I lay down any tape, but especially the plastic tape, there can't be a lot of tension in the tape. You have to relax the tape before you stick it down. One of the things I'm going to do is open the hood and continue the stripe down the front of the hood.

*Once I have a shape that I like, I check the dimensions...*

*... so I can duplicate the stripe on the other side.*

*Quarter inch masking tape is my tool of choice for the basic layout.*

I use a razor blade to cut the tape where it bridges the hood gap. This area will be masked off later.

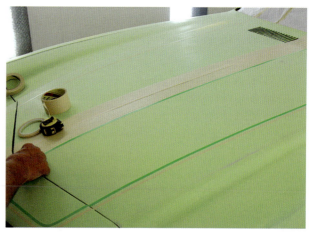

Here you can see how I've run the green plastic tape along the inside of the crepe masking tape. This will form a thin stripe on the inside edge of the layout.

After defining the stripe with the quarter inch masking tape I go along the inside...

It's important to mask this gap at the front of the hood.

...with quarter inch plastic tape. This material must be laid down without a lot of tension or it will pull away from the body later.

Initially I lay out the stripe on the back to the same dimensions as those used on the hood...

We try measuring the back stripes on the trunk the same as the front, then pull some tape and assess whether or not we like the shape. But it looks like it's too broad in the back, so we pull another piece of tape. The tape is easily fixed. Sometimes you have to follow your eye, not the tape measure. I like the narrower rear stripe better and that's how we're going to do it.

After doing the shape I like with the guide tape, I come in with the 1/4 inch plastic tape and pull the guide tape. Like the hood, I want to cut the tape where the trunk meets the body, then open the trunk and tape the opening. Next we mask off the car with 16 inch paper, this is the minimum I use in an application like this. While I'm doing the masking I like to push down on all the tape edges to be sure it's all stuck down well.

Now I want to wipe it down with a rag lightly dampened with final wash. I couldn't decide whether or not to continue the stripe over the top of the car, the Yenkos didn't. But once I do decide to stripe the top, the first thing I do is find the center. I use measurements transferred from the hood and trunk lid. The rest of the striping is easy.

Once we have the tape on the roof, I like the overall effect but it looks too narrow at the rear. Again, this is the time to critique the job, before you start painting. It's back to trusting your eye. I

*But the initial design looks too broad in the back.*

*So we lay it out again by eye and I like the results much better.*

*Like the hood I have to mask the trunk gap.*

51

*Sheets of masking paper are my choice for masking off the rest of the car.*

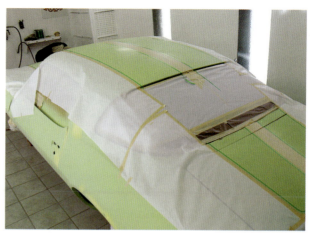

*Laying out the stripe across the top is relatively easy and then I can mask off the rest of the car.*

*Including the area on either side of the trunk.*

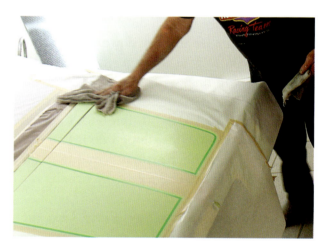

*We have to wipe the car down again with KC 20*

*Sometimes it's easier to really see the design with the masking paper in place. In this case I decide to stripe the roof as well as the hood and trunk.*

*You don't have to use the sealer as it comes out of the can, it's a good idea to mix colors to create a color close to the basecoat that will follow.*

decide to re-tape and this time I taper the tape only 1/2 inch as it comes to the back of the car.

Now I wipe it down with KC 20 cleaner, it's so important to clean the car and get rid of anything that might interfere with the paint's ability to adhere to the car. We still have to tack and blow off the car, then we're ready to paint.

## DIFFERENT BASES - DIFFERENT SEALERS

It's important to use a sealer with a color close to the basecoat. Under the black diamond we're using on the top of the car I use black, KS 11 sealer, mixed with KU 150, (though you can also use the KU 100). Sealers sometimes settle out, when I open one of the cans it turns out there are lumps on the bottom, the only way to get this done is to mix it. A lot of painters fail right here on the paint bench.

In this case I use one coat of sealer. First I check the pattern, in this case I want a six inch fan six inches from the surface, I don't need an 8 inch fan and I don't want to get more than five or six inches away from the car.

## PAINT THE TRUNK, TOP AND HOOD

After applying the sealer I tack it again, then mix the black diamond, MBC 03, two parts paint to one part reducer, without any catalyst. I've decided to use half 311, medium reducer, and half 310, fast reducer, because things are drying too

*Air and tack is the last step before application of the basecoat...*

*...except that I like to check the pattern to make sure it's 6 inches wide 6 inches from the surface.*

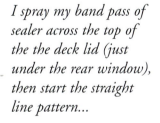

*I spray my band pass of sealer across the top of the the deck lid (just under the rear window), then start the straight line pattern...*

...moving up and down the trunk lid with 50% overlap between each pass.

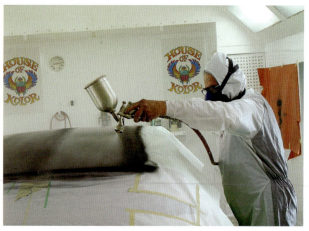

To apply the metallic basecoat I want a six inch fan not more than six inches from the surface. If you move too fast roughness can occur.

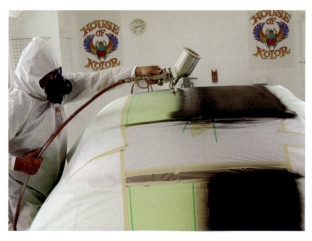

When the right side is finished I move to the left, applying sealer first to the hood, then the top and finally the trunk.

Straight lines, you've got to follow straight lines when applying any paint.

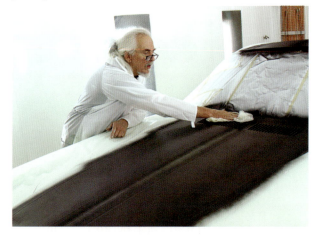

After applying a single coat of sealer I still have to tack the job before application of the basecoat.

The overlap between each pass is 75% with a flake material. I put on a total of 3 coats of the basecoat.

fast in the booth (it's over 80 degrees in the shop this day). Because of the metallic I sometimes use a bigger tip, but looking at this paint I'm going to stay with the 1.3 tip on the DeVilbiss Plus gun. I will open up the pattern a little though.

## PAINT THE SIDES

We are using platinum on the sides, MBC 02. The color is silvery gray, so we need a sealer that's just a little darker. I decide to try metallic sealer KS 12 darkened with black sealer, KS 11, under the platinum. The mixing ratio is 4:1:1 (this is catalyzed material). As always, I do a test panel first to check the fan. After putting on one coat I can see that to get nice even coverage without any blotching I will have to put on 2 coats of sealer.

After the second coat of metallic sealer we have to kill a little time and let that flash. If we put the basecoat on too soon it will lift and we don't want that. If we wait too long the base will be too dry which can cause delamination.

The platinum basecoat is a 2:1 mix ratio, without any catalyst. We're putting on three coats of platinum, MBC 02. For this I'm going to use a 1.5mm tip and choke it up a little bit, the paint has to stick to the sides, that's where it doesn't want to go. You can't wait too long to pull the tape. Especially when it's hot the tape can get

*Now I tape off the bottom panel, using the body line as the color break.*

*After masking off the upper body and tacking the surface we're ready for the sealer.*

*The gray sealer is a special mix (see the text).*

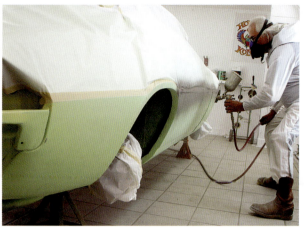

*When painting the sides you have to keep moving, you have to walk the car without stopping...*

*The basecoat MBC 02 is next. Overlap between coats should be 75%.*

*...while keeping the gun 90 degrees to the surface.*

*I put on a total of 3 coats of the platinum basecoat, allowing each coat to flash before applying the next.*

*Sometimes it takes two coats of sealer to get nice even coverage.*

*I pull the paper right away. At this point you can really see the design. And we still have to apply the pale gold to the main upper body.*

really hard to take off. It can also transfer the adhesive to the primer if it's left on too long.

## REVERSE TAPE

At this point we have to reverse tape all the areas we painted yesterday. On the narrow stripes I use 1/4 inch masking tape, and then I use wider tape and paper to mask off the rest. What I want on these areas that I reverse tape is to see a hairline of black showing through, it tells me I'm right. That way I know I won't have any of the primer showing through when the job is finished.

I use regular masking tape on the upper areas, but at the break line on the side of the car I use plastic tape, because the paint is going to be running downhill and it will want to creep under the edge of the tape. The plastic tape stands up better to the paint in these situations than the crepe tape. With the plastic tape I like to hold the roll quite a ways out in front of me and guide it with one hand while I push it down with the other. After I have the plastic tape in place I mask off the rest of the lower panels with paper.

Now I wipe the car down with two rags. I tell people, 'never wet more than you can wipe off before it dries.'

*We start reverse taping with conventional masking tape…*

*…though I use paper for the larger areas and plastic tape on the sides.*

*The sealer goes on with a DeVilbiss Plus gun and a 1.3 tip. It takes two medium coats to get good coverage.*

*The sealer we mixed matches the MBC color so well it's hard to tell one from the other.*

*It also helps to pull the tape sooner rather than later.*

*It takes 3 coats of the pale gold MBC to get good coverage.*

*The paint always rises up where it meets the tape edge, the dull knife blade knocks down that edge.*

*It's important to pull ahead and away from the paint to avoid pulling paint off the car.*

*A wipe down with a Scotch-brite pad is the next step before application of the kandy paint.*

## The Third Basecoat

Before applying the gold metallic basecoat, MBC 01, I have to put down a sealer that matches the basecoat. To create sealer of the right color I start with white sealer, KS 10, and add Spanish gold kandy concentrate KK 14 to get a gold look similar to the basecoat.

That doesn't work, the color is too yellow. So instead I try KS 12 metallic sealer with some of the KK 14 Spanish gold intensifier. This gives me a nice pale gold color that's just a little darker than the metallic base, which is exactly what I'm after. I tell people it's not a bad thing to make a mistake once in while, you need to experiment and try new things.

The mixing ratio for this is 4:1:1 again. I'm using KU 150 catalyst and RU 310 reducer, with just a little 311 because the temperature in the shop is over 80 degrees. The gun I'm using is a DeVilbiss gravity feed HVLP with a 1.3mm tip.

Before applying this base we have only to tack and blow the car. I'm using a six inch pattern six inches from the car. For the sealer coat you just need good coverage, if you get it covered in one you're done, but you seldom do. Usually it takes two coats. The 1.3 tip works really well with this Plus gun from DeVilbiss, if it were any bigger I would have mottling, and I don't. The sealer turned out so well you could almost use that as the base.

The mix for the basecoat is 2:1 we are using all 310 without any 311 because I want to move fast on this. The basecoat can be applied in about 60 minutes, though a fast reducer or warm temperatures can speed this. When I walk the car I always do one band pass at the top of the color break, but after that I use straight line techniques, which means that sometimes I don't go the full length of the car because the panel turns down. After applying the basecoat I apply a coat of SG 100 to protect the paint. In fact, I put a coat of SG 100 on each of the basecoats.

## Pull Tape and Paper

When pulling tape it's important to pull ahead and away from the car so you create that shearing

*Here I'm blowing off the car, and I still have to wipe it down and go over the surface with a tack rag. KC 20 is the only final wipe that won't harm the bases.*

*Even after all these years I try to be very precise and careful in my gun setup. For the kandy paint I want a 6 inch fan 6 inches from the car.*

*A stool is very helpful, this one has 2 steps and a hoop to lock your knees into. I like to start on the roof with my straight line technique.*

*Here you can see again how I keep each pass straight…*

*…and evenly spaced from the one before, with 75% overlap on the first 3 coats.*

*Next I move to the other side of the roof, using the same techniques.*

*It takes discipline and practice to keep the gun-to-surface distance the same and the gun always aimed 90 degrees to the panel.*

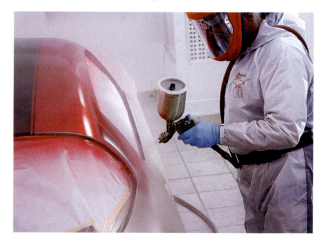

*The roof support is done is a series of quick passes.*

*Then I move right back to the top of the quarter panel.*

action. After I pull the tape I run a dull knife blade along the edge where the paint rises up to meet the tape, the blade knocks the edge down so you can't even feel it afterwards.

After going over all the taped edges with a dull knife blade I wash the whole car with a gray scotch brite pad and water. This eliminates lumps that form around any standing flakes and will save me time and trouble later.

Now I like to blow the car off, to get rid of any loose metallic flakes or dust that might fly up while we're painting. In fact, I'm going to re-paper the windows so I trap any loose material that might be clinging to the cardboard or tape. Then we need to clean the surface, but I can't use a solvent on a basecoat. I put some of the KC 20 on a rag and wipe down the whole car. I like this final wash from House of Kolor because it won't damage the basecoat.

## KANDY PAINT

The kandy color we're using here is a mix of kandy brandywine and kandy apple red, UK 01 and UK 11. The mix is one part brandywine and two parts kandy apple red. Brandywine is one of the nicest candy colors to work with. We're using KU 100 catalyst and 310 reducer. I might use a little 311 if it starts to dry too fast on me.

The test spray or pattern check is very important when it comes to shooting candies. My rule of thumb is a six inch fan six inches from the car. I'm using a 1.3mm tip in the Plus gun.

My first step is a 3:1 mix of the two kandies, I mix two buckets of this so I don't have to mix any in the middle of the paint job. I'm using a 2:1:1 ratio with two ounces of extra reducer per sprayable quart in the first coat for extra flow. I changed to a 1.2mm tip part way through the job because I could see pulsing in the pattern.

We did six coats of kandy total, then put on two coats of clear right away, UC 35. I don't over-reduce this clear, I mix it just the way the directions suggest.

*From the top of the quarter I just continue on to the right side of the trunk lid, then the panels on the very back of the body.*

*Note that there is no blotching or streaks even on the first coat of kandy. Proper gun techniques and a 75% pattern overlap make it happen.*

*The gun is a DeVilbiss Plus HVLP gun with a 1.2 tip. The large fittings and 40 feet of 3/8 inch hose provide enough air to achieve excellent atomization.*

*The hood requires a series of passes before I can move to the other side.*

*Areas like the bottom of the quarter panel require a series of separate passes.*

*From the left side of the hood I just make the transition to the Camaro's left side.*

*While the larger areas along the side require that you walk the car.*

*The idea is to keep moving, to be as efficient as possible. To make this profitable you have to move fast and get the work done.*

*After one complete coat the car looks great, but we're going to put on another 5 coats, which will give it a richer, darker tone.*

*Not all sandpaper is created equal. This "Cami" grade or P paper is manufactured in Europe and uses more consistent grain sizes than most American papers.*

*There are two coats of clear on top of the kandy paint, and we will only be sanding on this surface, never on the color.*

*I sand until most of the orange peel is gone, then I finish by hand.*

## COLOR SANDING/ HOOD DEMO

I start off sanding the hood by machine (the Bulldog) with a 600 grit dry pad. This really speeds up the process. Then I switch to using 500 grit wet, by hand, I like to put a tiny bit of Ivory liquid in the water, there's always a little stiction between the fresh paint and the sand paper, the Ivory acts as a lubricant so the paper really slides over the surface. It's important to use a red squeegee, because the black ones sometimes leave streaks on the paint.

You only want to sand on the clearcoat. Any time you see colored water, that

*We are using a 600 grit paper on this flat-sanding Bulldog. Each pad is good for about half a hood, before losing its bite.*

*When the sandpaper picks up a seed it will leave a tell-tale trail that looks like a coil spring.*

*This is a short demonstration of how effective wet sanding can be. Note the small blemish left behind by the dry sanding.*

*By cleaning the pad on a piece of gray Scotch-brite material I can eliminate the seed and continue using the sanding pad.*

*I using a flexible sanding pad and a piece of 500 grit paper.*

*Before moving on to wet sanding I like to wipe off all the dust left by the earlier steps.*

*The squeegee you use needs to be red rubber, not black, the black ones can leave streaks behind.*

means you've broken through to the paint and it's time to slow down. I wet sand an area, squeegee it off, look to make sure the shine is all gone, and then move on to the next area. If the paint is still shiny you haven't done your job.

Note the picture of the swirls in the paint that look like a coil spring (page 64). The swirls mean we have a seed on the disc and it's leaving the pattern. I use a number 7445 scuff pad from 3M to wipe the face of the sanding pads. This eliminates the seeds or burrs on the disc.

When I have most of the orange peel gone that's when I stop, it's best to do the rest by hand. Each pad seems to be good for about half a hood, then they loose their cutting power.

You can see the photo of the two small hickies just behind the headlight. The dry sanding knocks part of it down but does not eliminate the imperfection in the paint.

After wiping the area down to pick up residue with damp rag I start wet sanding. Note how the two small hickeys are completely eliminated by wet sanding with a small sanding block and some 500 grit paper.

## FINAL WIPE DOWN

When all the sanding is finished it's time for the final wipe down and for this I like to use clean water. I start with two rags, one wet, but not dripping, with water, and the other dry. I go over all the edges under the hood and the door jambs first, so there isn't any loose dust to fly up while we paint. Then I go over the whole car, first wiping an area, then wiping it dry. You have to be sure there aren't any areas where the water won't stick because if the water won't stay there neither will the paint. And of course you can't touch the surface with your bare hands or arms.

## FINAL CLEARCOAT.

For the final clearcoat we're using UFC 35, flow clear. This product has a little longer cure time but a higher gloss and it's easier to buff. I mix it it 2:1:1-1/2, heavy up on the reducer. I put on three coats total. One bond coat and two super-wet coats, all are mixed using 311 for the reducer (the shop temperature is 88 degrees on this day).

*After drying you can see the blemish is completely eliminated.*

*Eventually I do the whole car, first with 600 grit dry and then with 500 grit wet.*

*Now I do the final wipe down with clean water, if the water won't stick to an area, neither will the paint. When I find an area where the water won't stick I just sand again lightly and wipe again.*

*Just before application of the final clearcoat I like to blow off the car, then go over it with a tack rag.*

*The clearcoat we're using is UFC 35. Note how the stool I'm using gives me the height I need and also keeps my paint suit away from the car.*

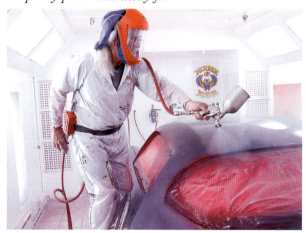

*I'm following the same pattern I established when I shot the primer, always using straight line techniques.*

*The pattern overlap for the clear is 50%. This is the same DeVilbiss HVLP gun I used earlier, in this case I'm using the 1.4mm tip.*

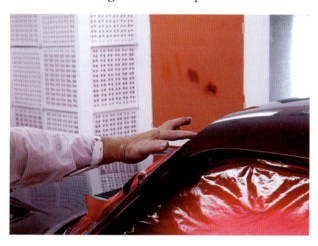

*When the paint has dried enough that it does not string up on my finger, I can apply the next coat.*

*I put on 3 coats of clear, one bond coat and two super wet coats.*

## CUT AND BUFF

A couple of days have gone by before we get to this stage, which is good because any shrinkage that is going to take place has already occurred.

There is new technology available that shortens the time it takes to polish a car. This involves the new sander we've already seen and some very good polishing compound

The heart of this new system is the flat-sanding DA. These new single orbiting dual-action sanders don't rock, they sand perfectly flat.

I start off with a 1000 grit dry pad on the sander and use very light pressure to eliminate any dirt nibs. Once I've gone over the hood with the 1000 grit, being careful to avoid the edges, I switch to 1200 and go over the entire hood again. This is the one time you can use your hand on the car. I need to wipe off the debris, between each step.

### Sanding Sequence

The next step is to use 2000 grit on the Dynabrade sander. The nice thing about this sander is the fact that we can use water to flush the debris away and keep the pad cool for longer life.

You need to squeegee the water off, then I like to wipe it with a rag because there are irregularities that you can't dry with the squeegee.

By doing it this way the buffing takes almost no time because you've already done most of the work. Then finish sand wet with 3000 to 4000 grit and the finish begins to shine - and you haven't even buffed yet.

### Buffing

For buffing I like a slow turning buffer, 1500 to 1750 rpm. It works better if you slow down the buffer and just let the compound do its work. 3M says up to 1750 RPM but no more.

You don't want to work a large area, it's better to work a small area as that generates a certain amount of heat. The idea is to reheat and flow the paint. The secret with rubbing compounds is to avoid using too much. You need to spread it at low RPM, then flatten the buffer and apply pressure and work the area back and forth.

*Here I'm working with the same Dynabrade I used earlier equipped with 1000 grit paper. This speeds the flattening of the art work edge.*

*After wiping off the car I will go over it one more time with 1200 grit on the same sander.*

*The Dynabrade is equipped with two "lines," one is connected to the air supply, the other to a bucket of water.*

I go over the whole car with the wet sander. The combination of a flat-sanding DA type sander and water means this step goes very fast.

I like to stay in one small area to create a certain amount of heat.

The squeegee is the best way to get all the water off the car.

The pad I'm using is cut-pile wool. Like sanding, the buffing is done in stages with different tools and materials.

The buffer I'm using turns at a relatively slow RPM, the compound is part of the Perfect-It III system from 3M.

The final step in the buffing sequence is application of glaze using the same buffer but a convoluted pad.

For the buffing pad you want cut pile wool, you don't want the ones that aren't cut because they can burn the paint and don't bring up the shine as quick as the cut ones do.

It's better to do a couple of applications of compound than to put on too much at once, with too much it tends to plug up the pad and it just doesn't want to go away.

We need to put the convoluted pad, or a foam pad, on the buffer for the glaze, but first I have to wipe it down. It's always a good idea to clean off any residue from the last step before going on to the next. For wiping down between glazing or buffing sessions I like the micro fine polishing cloth. It won't scratch at all and there aren't very many things you can say that about. The pictures probably explain the whole process better than I can.

When it comes to buffing products, I like the Perfect-It III system from 3M for buffing, though there are other good systems as well. System One is one of those. It's a new product built around a single compound with different pads for the polish and glaze steps.

With the available new technology and materials you can buff a whole car in about 6 hours. Normally that's about a 12 hour deal.

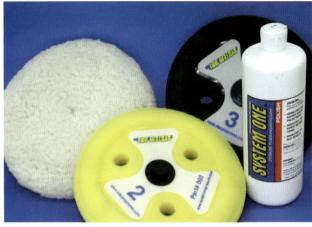

*There are a number of good buffing products on the market, including this complete kit from System One developed by a former body man.*

*When I'm finished the car has a very bright, very flat surface. The colors don't really show correctly until we have the car outside.*

*A great paint job with high gloss shows off the body work. That's why painting is as much about the preparation as it is about the actual application of the paint. A super straight body and deep-gloss paint job are the reward for a great job done with pride.*

# Chapter Five

# Super Bright Sporty

## A Multi-Level Layout

The parts seen here are all part of an Evo Sportster owned by Patty Mesenbrink of Brooklyn Park, Minnesota. We painted this bike once before, the idea this time is to update her machine with a fresh design. Painting the frame and the engine is so much work that Patty would like to avoid that step. My goal then is to pick colors that work with the existing blue frame and hot pink engine. Even though we are painting the entire bike the photos focus on the gas tank.

*This "before" picture shows the Sporty with the earlier paint job. For the new paint job we wanted to use colors that would work with the colors on the frame and engine.*

70

## STRIP THEN FILL

Before starting on the parts we sent everything out to Kirby's Custom Paint and Precision Paint Removers. Kirby is a master with the media blaster. On the fiberglass fenders he was able to strip off the paint without removing the original primer! He has amazing control.

The tank is an aftermarket Sportster tank with a raised section along the middle originally done in Donnie Smith's shop. Our first job is to get all the parts, including the side covers, ready for the first coat of primer. The tank must be molded all along the area where the raised section meets the top of the tank and in a few low areas. I don't like to just throw lots of plastic filler at a piece of sheet metal. I call it the thinking man's way of using filler. I tell people, 'fill the low spots, then sand that area, then fill again and sand again.'

When we add hardener to the filler it's important that the plastic tray we work on be totally clean of old filler. I like to mix the hardener and the filler thoroughly. After the filler is mixed I use a small flexible applicator and apply the filler to all the areas around the center of the tank, and to the front and back of the tank.

We don't wait for the filler to dry, but start working as soon as it's about half hard. The tool I like for a job like this is the half-round cheese grater.

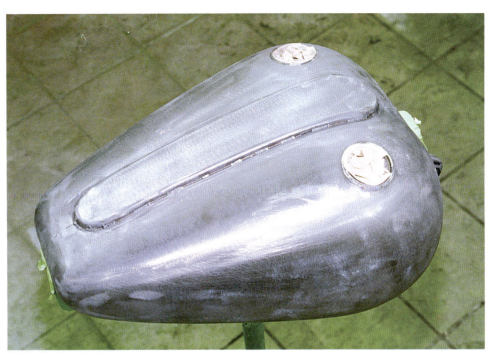

It's nice to start on bare metal whenever possible. In this case we had the parts media blasted to remove all the paint. Unlike sand blasting, media blasting can be done without warping the metal or damaging the surface.

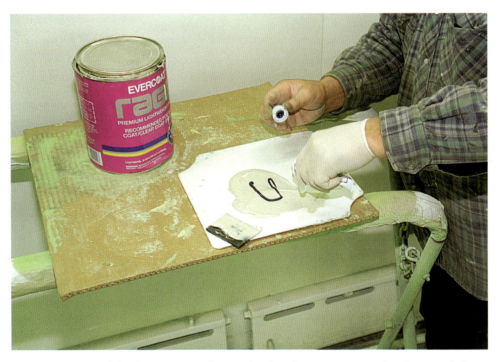

I'm always careful when mixing the mud: The plastic tray must be clean and the two materials must be well mixed before application

To make sure the filler and hardener are well mixed I use light and heavy strokes until the color is uniform.

The first application goes on where the raised section meets the tank.

The top of the raised panel is actually a little concave, so I try to fill that along with all the other obvious low areas.

You save so much time by working the filler before it's fully hard. I like to put on only as much filler as I need and no more.

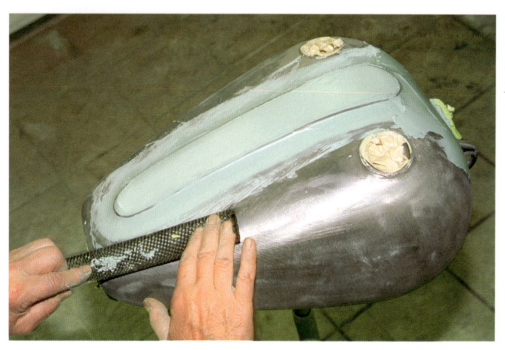

You can see from the photos how well it works on the filler before it's fully set up. After going over most of the tank with the cheese grater I wait a little bit for the filler to set up more, then start working with the small half-round sanding block. The sanding block is equipped with a sheet of 40 grit paper but at this point we could even be working with 36 grit. When you work with any sanding block it's important to cross-block. By sanding first in one direction and then at 90 degrees to that direction you avoid leaving a sanding pattern in the filler, and you also get a better reading on the condition of the filler. Next I use a small conventional sanding block on the flat areas.

During seminars I tell painters, 'the filler talks to you if you listen. It will tell you where the next application should go.' At this point I can clearly see where the low spots are because of the difference in the color of the filler. Before adding the next coat of filler though I always take some sand paper and scuff the filler in the low areas. There have to be scratches even in the low areas or the next application of filler won't stick. When I sand those low areas I move the sand paper in a different direction than I did in the area around the low area so it looks different and helps me to identify those low areas. Before applying more filler it's important to blow off all the dust, or it will interfere with the adhesion of the next coat of filler.

*With the half-round cheese grater you can carefully shave off the high spots...*

*...working first along the edges of the raised area and then onto the top.*

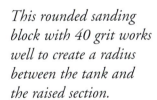

*This rounded sanding block with 40 grit works well to create a radius between the tank and the raised section.*

*It's important to check your work as you go. This is actually better done with a glove or rag which increases sensitivity and protects against transfer of oils.*

*A small sanding block and more 40 grit is the next step in the process.*

*Now I'm knocking down the high spots on the flattest parts of the tank.*

## SECOND APPLICATION OF FILLER

Now I mix up another small batch of filler and carefully apply it to the low areas. Once that filler has set up I use the DA with a 40 grit pad attached. Like I said before, I'm not opposed to the use of machines. It's not enough to be a good bodyman, you have to be a fast bodyman. Speed is important, time is money.

What we're trying to do at this point is knock down the high spots and bring the low spots up to level. When I'm done with the DA I get out the sanding blocks again, still equipped with 40 grit paper. And if I discover a big high spot, I just get out the machine again. I think one of the mistakes that painters make is they try to go too fine too quick with their sanding. Our primer will fill 24 grit scratches with two coats, you don't really need to go to fine paper before the primer.

There's still one small low spot on the right side of the tank and another at the very front so before applying the primer I put just a little more filler on those two areas. Finishing these areas follows a familiar pattern: first a little work with the cheese grater, then the DA and finally a flat sanding block.

## PRIMER

The primer I want to use here is the KP 2 CF. This is a chromate-free, fast-build primer. In the past our paints used Zinc Chromate to promote adhesion and help the product to withstand hours and hours of abuse in the salt-spray test cabinet. Because of environmental concerns the new primer uses Zinc Phosphate instead, and the test pieces still withstand over 1000 hours in the salt-spray cabinet with no breakdown or evidence of corrosion. The new formula also works just as well on aluminum and galvanized metal as the old one did.

Before applying the first coat of primer we blow off the parts and then wipe them down good with acetone, GON or KC 20. The acetone works good on the parts that are bare steel.

It's important to tape over the gas tank opening, including the very edge of the opening where the cap seals. In other words, you want the seal from the cap to sit on bare metal. If the seal sits on a coat of paint the gas fumes will eventually seep up under the paint and cause a blister at the opening.

At this point we need at least one more coat of filler, and it's not too hard to see where.

To speed things up I start in with the DA and a 40 grit pad.

I start the second application of filler in the radiused area at the edge of the raised area...

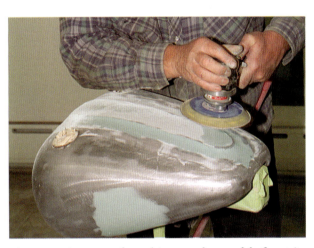

Again, we've started working on the mud before it's fully hard.

...then add some to the low areas on the flat sections.

To finish forming the radius I use the rounded sanding block, still wrapped in 40 grit.

This third application of filler is used to fill a low area on the right side.

Before applying primer, I'm going to re-tape the gas tank opening.

The front of the tank is fairly flat - a good spot to use the cheese grater before the mud is fully hardened.

The tank needs to be clean so the primer is sure to stick to the metal.

## Apply The Primer Surfacer

The primer is put on with a SATA HVLP gun running at 37 psi at the gun. We start on the areas that are covered with filler, then move over the rest of the parts. After that first coat on the filler areas has flashed we go back in and apply a second coat of primer. We will continue to apply more primer after the previous coat has flashed, until we have a total of five coats on the filler areas and three on the areas that were bare metal.

Once all these coats are applied we need to let the parts sit for fourteen hours before we can begin to block sand. The total time will depend on the temperature of the booth of course, we like to work in a minimum of 70 degrees.

## Guide Coat Number One

At this point the tank has a total of 5 coats of primer on the areas with filler and 3 on what were the bare metal areas. Now we are going to put on a light mist of dark grey lacquer primer (page 78). This light coat is our guide coat. A guide as to how flat the paint is and where we might have a low spot that needs a little spot putty for example.

Next we come in with a DA, equipped with 240 paper. You could also do with this a flexible pad however, with either 240 dry or 400 wet. The 240 paper on the DA will flatten the primer and show up the low spots.

The first few passes with the DA show up some low spots on the top of the tank. Now we will do more sanding with the DA to see if we can eliminate the low spots before we break through into the metal underneath.

## Spot Putty

To fill those small low areas we use catalyzed spot putty, this is a two-part polyester glazing putty from Evercoat (page 78). It's important to knead the hardener first, before putting it on the plastic mixing surface. Extra material can be cut off with a half-round file.

Now we will finish the areas where we applied the spot putty with an 80 grit Hookit disc from 3M. On the tank we start by feathering the edges with the mini DA then we work our way across the center of the raised section. It should be pretty close now, but if there's a little high or low spot showing that's probably OK because we're going to apply

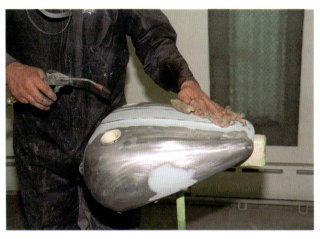

*The very last thing I do before applying the primer is air and tack.*

*The gun is a SATA HVLP dedicated primer gun. The idea is to put more primer on the areas with filler than the areas that are bare steel.*

*We've put 5 coats on the areas with filler, the primer needs to cure 12 to 14 hours before we can start sanding. To cure correctly the booth needs to be at least 70 degrees.*

77

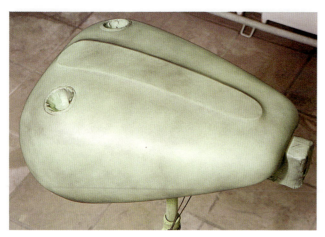

At this stage we've applied the guide coat and the sanding can begin.

We're going to start on the tank with a DA and some fairly fine, 240, grit paper.

Whether you're mixing filler or spot putty, the plastic pallet needs to be clean of all the old filler.

It's important to knead the hardener before mixing the two-part spot putty.

another 3 coats of primer. This is why we don't fill the small low areas along the top of the tank on either side, because I'm sure those will sand out.

At this time we smooth out the radius to the raised area with 80 grit, working by hand. We will leave the area with 80 grit scratches as our primer will easily fill those scratches (not shown). First we feather the edge where the filler meets the paint. Then we flatten the whole area where we applied the filler.

You have to be very careful anytime there's an edge, like on the side cover. We sand "over the edge" at an angle, rather than along the edge the long way. We finish blocking out the tank with 80 grit on the small hand pad. Now we can prime the bottom of the tank and then put additional primer on the top where we were block sanding yesterday, using the same primer as last time.

For getting up into the recesses in the bottom of the tank I choke the gun up (with the fan con-

Here you can see the low spots on the top of the tank.

To be absolutely certain the raised area is flat, we hit it with a sanding block and 400 grit paper.

We put the spot putty on quick, and carefully, to the low areas on the top of the tank...

We do the final finishing of the radius by hand.

...then sand right away with 80 grit on the mini DA.

Items with edges, like this side cover, must be sanded and finished carefully. We always do the edges by hand.

*At this point we primer the bottom of the tank, with the gun adjusted to a dot pattern...*

*...and re-primer the top of the tank as well.*

*After allowing the primer to cure we do a guide coat and then start block sanding. I like to soak the paper for 20 minutes before sanding begins.*

trol knob), which turns the pattern to a dot instead of a fan. That way it does a better job of covering those areas. You have to be careful though because you're putting on more paint and it's more likely to run with the gun set this way.

Now we flip it over and start by putting primer on the center section, where we put the fresh filler. After that flashes we put primer on the rest of the tank. We will put another three coats on, with two extra coats on the body worked areas, so a total of five coats on areas like the top. After application of all that material the primer needs to cure overnight.

## GUIDE COAT NUMBER TWO

We do a guide coat of lacquer, just a mist coat like before. We spray this on and then let it dry, which it does very quickly, then we can start in sanding again with 400 grit wet, with no soap. The idea at this point is to take out the scratches. We start on the top of the tank with a flexible sanding block wrapped in 400 grit paper. Then I do the rest of the tank with 400 on the palm of my hand. There's so much curve to the tank that it's hard to do this with a block.

It's important to avoid busting through the primer at this stage so we don't have to re-prime the tank. If we do sand through in one or two small areas the sealer/primer we're going to use will effectively act as primer in those small areas. We're flattening the primer. We continue to sand in a X-pattern, first one way and then the other. At this point the tank is essentially done. I have about 14 hours invested in body work and primer for all the parts.

## SEALER COAT

The white sealer, KS 10, is mixed 4:1:1 with KU 150 (KU 100 could be used as well) and RU 310 fast reducer. I decide to shoot with a Geo HVLP Gun. It's nice to have the gauge and additional regulator at the gun. Because of pressure drop through the hose, what you have indicated at the wall isn't what you have at the gun. The white sealer, KS 10, is the basecoat for the pearl. We don't have to use a separate basecoat. We save a step this way, though because we are using this as a basecoat I'm going to put on two coats.

It's important to re-tape the gas tank openings. We start by wiping off the bare metal edge with acetone, then we apply new tape. This way we keep

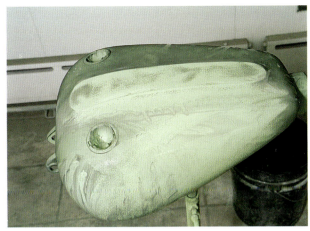

*The final sanding of the primer is done with 400 grit paper. The initial sanding shows up a few low areas.*

*The primer is thick enough though that most of the small low areas could be eliminated without breaking through the primer.*

*Gas tank openings need to be left bare at the very edge where the cap seals. If this bare edge is maintained the paint will not blister at the cap.*

*We re-tape the openings a number of times to be sure no dust is trapped in the tape. I also sand the edge of the primer so it doesn't get too thick.*

*Air and tack is always the last step before painting.*

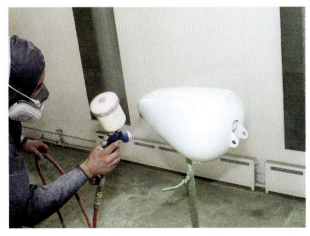

*The KS 10 sealer/basecoat is applied in 2 coats, the first coat needs to flash before applying the second.*

*Two coats gives us a nice foundation of basecoat for the colors to follow. If the sealer sits longer than 1 hour it's a good idea to sand with 500 grit.*

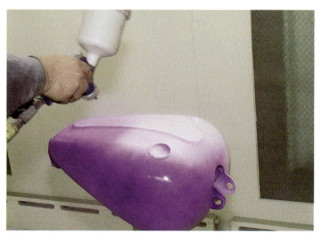

*This Shimrin shoots almost like a lacquer, it dries fast and the second and third coats go on quick. The Geo HVLP gun is adjusted to have 28 psi at the gun.*

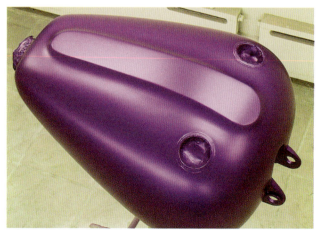

*I only have to wait 5 to 8 minutes between coats, the paint should not be sticky when the next coat is applied.*

paint from getting inside the tank, and ensure that the gas caps will seal against bare metal. It's a good idea to re-tape the stands that the parts are sitting on too because of dust that might have settled there. I wipe everything off with a warm rag damp with water. The last step is to blow and tack the tank before painting begins. I adjust the regulator to get 28 psi at the gun which is what they recommend. After the first coat flashes and looses its shine we put on the second.

### PEARL BASECOAT

You must wait at least one hour after applying sealer, before applying the first coat of pearl. If you wait longer than one hour the sealer must be sanded with 500 or 600 grit wet to create a mechanical bond. Before spraying any colored basecoat we knock down any nibs that stick up with 500 grit paper. This will eliminate any little nibs that might stick up above the color and show as white specs. Then we tack everything one more time.

The passion pearl PBC 65 is next. The paint finish will remain flat until the clearcoat goes on. On all the parts, especially the fenders, we're careful to get the paint up under the edge. We get paint up under the bottom of the tank, sometimes it helps to dial the paint nozzle to a dot, instead of a fan, and then spray areas like the tunnel of the gas tank that way.

After three coats of PBC 65 we clear the tank with UC 35. These three coats of clear are not over reduced or "flow coated" because we know we're going to sand on this material. You always have to apply some kind of clear over the color before you come in to do the taping and art work. SG 100 basecoat clear may also be used but it is not solvent resistant.

### COLOR SANDING

The color sanding starts with 500 grit paper wet (page 83). At this point we handle the parts with rags, so there are no oils transferred from our hands to the paint. It's a good idea to rinse and dry the tank often during the sanding, so you only sand the areas that are still glossy. With fiberglass fenders static electricity is a problem. It's better to blow the parts off or use a squeegee than to wipe it down with a rag. The wiping exacerbates the static problem.

The clear goes on in 3 coats. We start with a medium coat, then do 2 heavy wet coats with a ten minute wait in between each one.

After 3 coats of clear the parts have to sit for a minimum of 12 hours at a minimum of 70 degrees before we can sand with 500 grit

As always, first we move the sandpaper across the tank in one direction and then at 90 degrees to that direction.

To knock down the shine I'm using 500 grit paper though you could use 600 or 800 if you wanted. A little Ivory liquid in the water is a good idea.

I'm using a small, flexible sanding pad, though sometimes on a tank you have to work without a pad.

Areas like those around the gas cap filler must be done carefully by hand, otherwise the tank is ready for art work.

After cleaning I start laying out the design with tape. I prefer to work right on the tank.

The design evolves as I work. If there's an area I don't like, I just pull that section and do it again.

Here you can see the small piece of tape I use as a marker or guide on the tank's left side.

You do have to get the two halves of the tank the same. Both on the top and on the sides. That old line, "you can only see one side at a time" is a lame excuse. I check dimensions from one side to the other with a ruler or small tape.

## PLAYING WITH TAPE

I start this part of the project by wiping off the tank with KC 20 water borne cleaner. The layout or design is based on an illustration from a magazine. I lay it out free-hand with 1/8 inch crepe tape and use a ruler to make sure the two sides are identical. If I'm off a little on one side then I can make an adjustment. Usually I put a small piece of tape on the tank as a guide, and re-run the tape.

I like to use masking paper whenever I can, there's less chance to have a transfer of adhesive to the base coat. You need to use a urethane grade of masking paper, one that won't be soaked through during the painting process. The paper is available at any body shop supply store. There are many grades of paper, buy a good one. The paper is one of those little things that means a lot. Paper is cheaper than tape, but don't go too far and buy cheap paper.

When the taping is finished I give the tank a quick wipe down with KC 20, then a quick wipe with a tack rag just to get rid of any lint from the rags.

## COLORS

Strato blue, BC 04, is our first color. It should cover in two coats. I'm shooting it at 40 psi at the regulator with the trigger pulled, but it ends up taking three medium coats to get coverage (page 86).

*Once the design is finished I can finish up with paper rather than tape.*

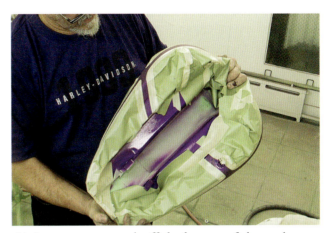

*It's important to mask off the bottom of the tank as well at the top.*

*I wipe the tank down with cleaner and then give it a quick once-over with the tack rag.*

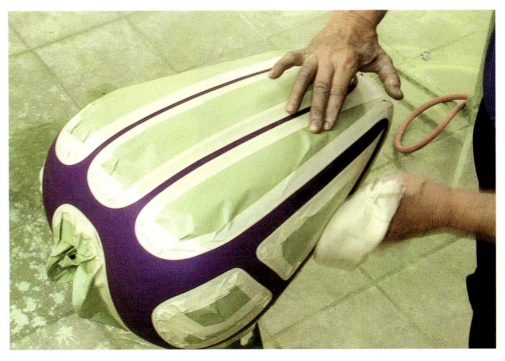

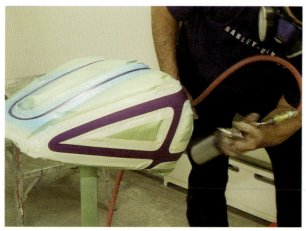

*I'm working with a touch up gun, we don't need a standard size gun in this situation.*

*The oriental blue kandy goes on in 3 quick coats, using the same touch up gun.*

*The first color we apply is strato blue. I only have to wait 5 to 10 minutes between the 2 coats - as determined by temperature and reducer speed.*

*The end color is a nice rich blue, a combination of strato blue base and a oriental blue kandy. Before pulling the tape I did one coat of SG 100.*

*I like to mix colors by eye and check the effect on the mixing spatula. Here I'm adding KK 04 to reduced SG 100 to make a low-solid basecoat kandy.*

*I want a clean break as I pull the tape in order to minimize the odds on pulling any paint.*

Next comes oriental blue, sprayed on top of the BC 04. This is a kandy color I mixed using KK 04 (kandy koncentrate) and SG 100. The SG 100 is thinned 100% (normal is 50%), the ratio of SG 100 and mixed KK is determined by eye (see the side-bar below). I apply three medium coats without much wait between coats. You're just looking for a dry touch before you put on the next coat. Then I apply one coat of straight SG 100 to protect the paint as soon as the last coat doesn't feel sticky on my finger.

*I'm using a gray scuff pad but 500 grit paper wet works better before striping and also serves to eliminate the edges.*

---

**Mixing Kandy Koncentrates**

The standard mixing ratio for mixing kandy koncentrates is 8:1, eight parts mixed SG 100 and one part KK. If you want a stronger color, try adding one to two ounces of KK per sprayable quart - always checking at each stage of mixing with a stainless steel spatula under a bright light.

---

Next we pull the tape. I always pull the fine line tape last. Pull it ahead and away from the paint, this creates a shearing action so you are less likely to pull the paint. Now we clean up any mis-tapes and over-spray areas. For this I like to use a gray Scotch-brite pad with water.

Water and a gray Scotch-brite pad takes off any little edges on the art work, or small high spots. People think it's going to take off paint but it won't, you don't have to worry. Some painters like to blow off the water, but sometimes I just use a rag to wipe off the water. For over-spray under the tank I like to use Acetone on a rag, but this only works when a catalyzed clear is used or the acetone will remove the basecoats!

*Over spray under the tank can be cleaned up with acetone, the rest is done with a Scotch-brite pad, note the warning in the text regarding the use of acetone.*

## MORE CLEAR COATS

Three coats of UC 35 clear come next, one bond coat and two wet coats. This will give us a thick enough surface that we can sand on the paint. With the shop at 70 degrees and a fast dry reducer I wait four to five minutes between coats. How long you wait will vary with the temperature of your shop and the amount of air movement.

*Before pinstriping the art we've just laid down I put on 3 coats of UC 35 clear.*

*After doing the pinstriping (not shown) I put on another 3 coats of clear UC 35.*

*...before deciding which design is the best.*

*When the clear is dry we can scuff the tank with 500 wet. The idea is to eliminate the stripe-bump and leave a surface the next coat will stick to.*

*Part of a good design is the fact that it will transfer to the other parts of the bike.*

*Now it's time for layout number two. As always, I often try more than one idea...*

*We have to keep track of which parts of the existing paint we want to preserve, which parts go "over" and which go "under."*

After the UC 35 has cured for at least 12 hours I can sand the clear with 500 grit wet, then lay down the pinstripes on the clear (page 88).

For the pinstriping I used our urethane light blue, U 9, striping paint and a 0000 brush. I always try to create a fine line, it adds to the detailing.

After the pinstriping it's time for three more coats of UC 35 clear, one bond coat and then two wet coats. With the booth at 70 degrees I waited five to eight minutes between coats. After the clear is cured I use wet 500 grit paper to knock down the striping bumps, you can use finer paper but it takes longer and the first coat of clear will fill these 500 grit scratches without any trouble. The idea is to sand until you can't feel the stripe. There should be no shiny spots left when you are finished.

## LAYOUT NUMBER TWO

When I'm doing a layout I don't draw things out, I just start taping. Once I have a rough idea of the layout I want on the tank, then I try the same thing on the fender and side cover so I know the design will transfer to the other parts. Some people use colored pencils or a sketch pad and that works for them. I like to work with tape right on the tank, I have the design and the colors in my head.

In laying the design out on the fenders you just have to try to keep the width of the lines even, judging it visually. After doing one fender that way I use it as the pattern for the other fender. Sometimes you just have to disregard the shape of the fender and do what looks right. In this case, for example, the fenders aren't exactly the same from one side to the other.

Now we finish taping out, note the tape on the center of the big panel on the side of the tank, this is where the new design will go "under" the existing artwork.

The white base coat, BC 26, is applied now. This will act as a brightener under the art work to follow. The base goes on in two light coats. After applying the base paint I need to wait 30 minutes before I can put down tape. You might be able to do it a little faster if you've used fast dry reducer and paid attention.

I start the tape-out for art on top of the white base with 1/8 inch crepe tape (page 90). The first piece of tape is put down just to find the center of

*Again, it's faster and cheaper to finish the masking with paper rather than tape.*

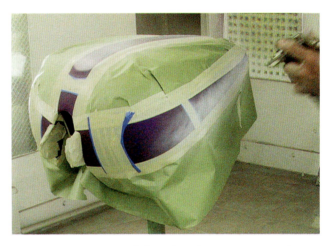

*Now comes 2 coats of the white basecoat, BC 26.*

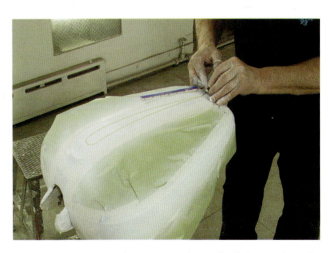

*I like to clean up the tape at the end of the oval with an X-acto knife.*

*Now I finish taping over the oval...*

*Parts of an old broom is what I use to make the mask, an idea I borrowed from airbrush artist Craig Fraser.*

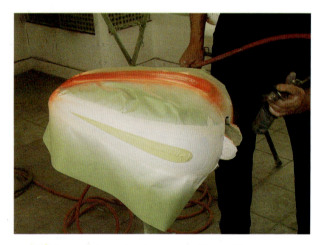

*...before applying the first coat of pearl basecoat with the touch up gun.*

*Then I spray a darker orange, ultra orange, through the mask on the top and the sides.*

*To get good coverage I put on two coats of the sunset orange.*

*And this is what it looks like after spraying. In hindsight a color with more contrast might have worked better.*

the panel. Then I tape out the oval panel. I do the same design on the top panel, and also on the other side of the tank.

I like to touch up the point of the tape with an X-acto knife, the oval will be pinstriped but you might as well make the line as clean as you can. On the left side of the tank I often measure to make sure the left side dimensions match what I've already done on the right side.

Some painters don't even worry if one side is different. But you've got to realize you're not just trying to please the customer. You have to please yourself - and everyone else who looks at the job. Critics are everywhere.

## MORE PEARLS

Now I put on two medium coats of PBC 31 sunset orange with the small touch up gun. Sometimes you have to try new things and for this I created a mask from straw.

The color I'm going to use with the mask is PBC 64 ultra orange, thinned 100% because you don't need a lot of color to come through. What I want is kind of a foggy effect. For this mask we had to try it a couple of different ways and angles until I got it the effect I wanted. We ran all the patterns in a horizontal direction, though you could make them more random if you wanted. I shot all of this at 25 psi with the touch up gun.

## THE DROP SHADOW

The drop shadow is done with SG 100 mixed one to one. After stirring it well I add small amounts of black, BC 25, you don't need a lot. The idea is to create a drop shadow. Every place the blue goes over orange, we do a drop shadow. Every place we had the tape out for that teardrop we do a drop shadow. It gives us that 3-D effect

I am using a special DeVilbiss gun made to do a dot pattern, this gun has no air horns. Note, a touch up gun adjusted to a dot pattern will do the same thing. After the shadows we need one coat of SG 100 applied before we pull the tape, this protects the fogging that we just did.

Now we can pull the tape, and even though we aren't done you can see it's starting to look like something. This is only fun when you shoot from the hip, when you can have some creative freedom. With the tape off you can start to see what it's

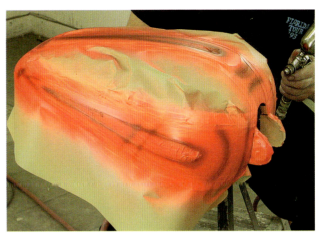

*Before pulling the tape I create a drop shadow. The paint is BC 25 jet set black mixed lightly with SG 100.*

*You can't really appreciate what's been done until you pull the tape.*

*A close up shows the effect of the mask and the drop shadow.*

91

*We're not done yet. We need to do more taping, being sure we don't tape over any of the white.*

*Then moving on to masking paper...*

going to be, I mean you have this idea in your head, as you pull the tape you have to ask yourself, 'is this what I was looking for?'

## TAPING OFF THE WHITE,

The idea here is to leave a little bit of the other color showing so we know we're getting complete coverage of the white. If this were not going to be pinstriped we would use the plastic tape, because that leaves a really clean line. You can't bend the tape as you put it on, or you get pockets.

Once the tape is applied to the edge of the white area then we change to the taping machine because it's faster and easier. I do some light scuffs and then touch up the white where we have nicks. If I'd have done SG 100 over the white I wouldn't have to do this.

The paint will be fogged onto the white oval, PBC 35 pink pearl surrounded by PBC 39 hot pink pearl. We spray the PBC 35 into the center of the spear with the small fogging gun, the regulator is adjusted to 35 psi at the wall with the trigger pulled. This is the gun we used earlier, it has no "horns" so only sprays a dot pattern. The color is built up over a series of passes down the center of the spear until I like the coverage and feel that it's even.

This gun puts on so little material that it might take 12 or 15 passes to get the color and coverage I want. At this point it's almost like using an airbrush.

*...before beginning the application of the two pink colors over the white basecoat, BC 26, laid down earlier. The first paint color is pink pearl sprayed into the center of the oval.*

As I look over the parts I can see the gas tank has more white showing through at the edge of the spear, so I take the gun with hot pink and put more on to darken that area. This is a good example of the kinds of adjustment you have to make when doing elaborate layouts. When I'm all done I grab the other gun and put on a light coat of SG 100.

Now, right after pulling the tape, it's a good idea to scuff the whole paint job with some worn out 500 grit sand paper and water. This will knock down the tape edges which makes it easier to get a perfectly flat surface later. All of this paint has been clearcoated otherwise you can't sand on the basecoats. Then I take a scuff pad, a gray Scotch-brite pad, with some water and go over everything one more time. This is when you want to look for any mis-tapes or areas that have to be touched up.

I doubled the reduction for fogging or blending, which will give me finer atomization and slower coverage. It means you make a lot of passes, but it's more forgiving of any little hiccup from technique or the gun.

Now we can put on two coats of clear, UC 35, one medium wet, one super wet, just enough that I have something to pinstripe on.

For this application I mixed up a special color, orange and red, and mixed them. It's what I would call vermilion. The ratio is two parts red U-3, to one part orange U-4.

*Next I surround the pink with hot pink PBC 39 applied with a touch up gun.*

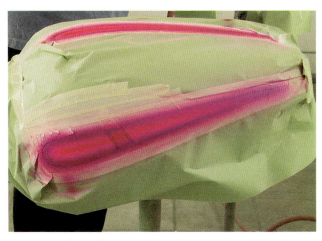

*Before pulling the tape I inspect the area just painted for complete coverage and consistent color.*

*Before pulling the tape I put on a quick coat of SG 100, just to protect the work we just did. Once the tape is pulled the tank looks pretty good but we aren't done yet.*

*Before pinstriping I apply another 2 coats of clear UC 35 and allow that to dry.*

*The clear is scuffed with 500 grit paper before I put the tape in place.*

## THE SECOND SET OF PINSTRIPES

The striping paint I'm using here is kosmic striping urethane. These striping paints are designed to be cleared. The other color is magenta UC 14 and lavender UC 15. By mixing them together I get a lavender that's pretty nice.

Scotch tape is really handy in some of these situations. I use it where one line crosses another. I like to use the number 811, the removable tape, because it doesn't leave any residue behind. And I make a little folded-over flap so there's a corner that you can grab when it's time to pull the tape.

You can use plastic masking tape, but you can see this so it's easy to cut without cutting the paint. It's an excellent product. And it's so thin your hand glides right over it. With masking tape you always get some creep under the edge of the tape.

The brush I'm using is a 000 size, made from natural bristle squirrel tail hair. You must pallet the paint when using the paint with U 00, the paint is designed for this. Some painters use fast dry reducer like 310, that's not designed for this, and then they have trouble as a result.

With pinstriping the more pressure you put on the brush the wider the line becomes. No one does a perfect line all the time, people shouldn't get too critical on their lines, it's human to have a little variation in the line.

*Notice how I started the line on the tape, then stopped on the next piece of tape. And started again on the tape. This way you get nice consistent lines. The tape is so thin you don't get a bump of any kind when the brush goes from tape to tank, or tank to tape.*

The tape allows you to start the line on the tape so that when the brush hits the actual line it's flowing along really nice. This paint dries so fast you can be in the booth in one hour applying the clear. You can make some money this way. One Shot isn't like that, it never dries that quick. And being oil-based it can lift when cleared.

When the orange is done I like to check all the areas I've painted before cleaning the brush. This paint can be wiped off with acetone if you make a mistake.

You can use any kind of coated paper or board for a palette, but it's best to use something that's coated so the paint won't soak into the paper.

Most pinstripers, me included, have trouble with the curves, You have to rotate the brush as you go. With our paint you can't tell where you start or stop the line. You can stop and take a call and then start over and you can't tell later.

You can use a liner brush for the tight corners, because striping brushes don't like to do tight turns. If you do, you have to be sure to rotate the brush as you go. It's a good idea to really load up the brush with paint before you start on a tight turn.

You can wipe off mistakes with a lightly soaked acetone rag, use firm pressure, then come back from the other direction and wipe off the little tail. Note: this can only be done when the striping is done over a catalyzed clear like our UC 35.

*With a complex design it's hard to get one pinstripe to stop exactly where the other one starts.*

*The tape allows me to do exactly that. The line where the two meet is nice and clean.*

*For pinstriping the sunrise and sunset colors I use the vermillion, mixed from red and orange striping paint. Note how the little finger of each hand is used to support the hand holding the brush.*

*Curves are among the hardest things to stripe. You have to roll the brush between thumb and forefinger as you go around the corner.*

*Straight lines are relatively easy, though a thin straight line still takes patience and practice.*

*The finished tank. Now you can see how the pinstripes help to define all the different sections and colors.*

You have to pay attention to the way the brush feels as you move it across the palette, if it feels stiff you know you aren't going to be able to get the paint off the brush and onto the tank.

You can keep the paint wet all day if you add U 00 and palette the brush until it loosens up again. Note that I keep the U 00 in a separate glass, so I don't dip the brush right into the paint can and contaminate it. A little corn starch on the hands is a good idea too, so your hands slide easily over the tank.

As we mentioned before, static is a problem with the fiberglass fenders, you have to be careful because the electrical charge wants to pull the paint right off the brush.

The lavender is the second striping paint I have to put down. Now all that's left is to touch up the blue pinstripes where the other colors cross, and then we can let everything dry and do the clearcoats.

As we've done in the past, I clearcoat over the stripes with UC 35, one bond coat and two wet coats. After that dries for 12 hours I flatten the paint with 500 grit paper using a flexible sanding pad, and in some cases, no pad at all.

For the final clearcoats I use UFC 35, this is our flow-clear, it's softer and easier to buff later. Again, I like to start with a light bond coat and follow that with two or three wet coats. In this case I used two wet coats. When I mix the clear for the flow coat I add a little extra reducer. The ratio I use is 2:1:1-1/2 (50% extra reducer).

Color sanding and buffing starts with the Bulldog and a 1500 grit pad. Wet sanding begins with the "wet" Dynabrade buffer. First a 2000 grit pad and then a 4000 grit pad. Buffing begins with a big variable speed buffer (you don't want to run over 1750 RPM), a cut-wool pad and some Perfect It III rubbing compound from 3M and progresses to the Perfect-It III machine glaze buffed with the convoluted foam pad.

A little Kosmic Shine, applied with a soft foam applicator and wiped off with a soft towel finishes the paint job.

*Before applying the last coat of clear, you need to carefully inspect the tank and all the stripes for any little mistakes or hiccups.*

*The finished job seen outside under a hazy sky. Note the way the design and colors work with the existing engine and frame colors.*

# Chapter Six

# Color-Change Flames on a Dyna

## Fix it, Then Flame it

Seen here is a paint job done on a Harley-Davidson Dyna that belongs to Shantha Jayapathy. Though we are painting the entire machine, we've decided again to focus on the gas tank. As with the other projects seen in the book, I decided to start by having all the paint and old mud stripped off so we are working on the bare metal. This is especially important in the case of the Dyna because the bike has had so much body work before.

The first thing I do after getting the parts in

*As I've said before, the paint job is only as good as the foundation, and you can't have a good foundation if you're painting over primer and body work of unknown quality.*

the shop is set the tank up on a nice sturdy stand. Whenever I can I like to wire the parts to the stands. There's nothing worse than having the tank or fender move during the painting - or fall off the stand.

I start by scuffing the tank with 80 grit paper. This cleans the metal and leaves a surface the filler can grab hold of. The stripping media that they use at Kirby's leaves a coating on that can inhibit the adhesion of the filler. For this first application I mix the mud a little light on hardener so I have more time to work. The filler I'm using is Rage Gold, I like it because it sands easily.

## FIX THE FIT

Now I coat the tank with the first coat of mud and set the dash down on the tank. I don't pull the dash until the mud is partially set up. The edge of the dash leaves a line in the filler, and I use a cheese grater to take the filler down to that line. What I'm really doing is a series of trial fits and grating sessions. Then I clean up the edges and scuff all the filler with 40 grit paper. This is important so the next coat of filler has something to stick to.

## A SECOND APPLICATION OF FILLER

For the next batch of filler I use just a little more hardener. With this application of mud I will blend in the filler we already applied with the surface of the tank and fill in the dents in the tank. It's always a good idea to make each application of

*After being stripped the tank and dash look a little rough. Note the gap where the dash meets the tank.*

*I like to set the dash down into the mud when it's still soft, then let it start to set up before pulling it.*

*Here we have a perfect imprint of exactly how much filler we need to fill the gap between dash and tank.*

99

The cheese grater is one of my favorite tools for situations like this. I'm working the mud before it's completely hard.

...and to begin filling the rough areas on either side of the tank.

A test fit shows improvement but we need a little more filler near the middle and back of the dash.

The cheese grater doesn't work very well on rounded corners...

The second application of filler is used to add height to the center of the tank...

...for the sides of the tank I like the six inch mud hog, in this case I'm using 36 grit paper.

filler as smooth as possible, there's no point in making any more work for yourself than necessary.

I pull the mud one way and then pull it the other, the mud goes the way you pull it. To center it over a low spot it's a good idea to pull it the other way on the last few pulls. You can do a lot with this filler when it's half-hard. Once it's fully hardened it's much tougher to sand and work. This is true of all the brands.

Cheese graters are good tools, they move the filler fast and they're less expensive than sand paper. You should treat these like sand paper in the sense that you should always work in an X-pattern.

The grater works like a long sanding block and a guide coat, when you're done with an area you can see the low spots easily. But for round areas like the front corners of this tank I like to use a mud hog with a 36 grit pad. I like the small one I'm using here, it's from National Detroit, a six inch model 9600. The pad rotates off-center like a DA, but this is faster than a DA, and does a better job of blocking. Unlike a DA the pad actually spins. To start working the mud I have a 36 grit pad on the sander.

I'm using a light touch, concentrating on keeping the pad flat to the surface so I'm only taking off the high spots. The key here is to let the mud talk to you.

I want to slow down what I'm removing so I switch to a sanding block. These blocks that I'm using allow you to pull the pins that run lengthwise and have the block contour to the surface, or leave the pins in for a more rigid sanding block.

Time to do another trial fit of the dash. I have to remember that the primer and the paint will add to the surface thickness, so there should be just a little space between the dash and tank. Before adding another layer of filler I have to scratch any un-sanded filler with 36 or 40 grit paper.

## THIRD AND FOURTH APPLICATION

The hardest thing to teach people starting out is to finesse the mud, if you do it saves you so much work. I have to wait until the mud is grate-able (page 102). Once I get close I don't use the mud hog anymore, it takes off too much too fast. I use either the DA or I do it by hand.

*This mud hog is a small model, a 6 inch from National Detroit. The pad rotates off-center like a DA, but it does rotate and it's faster than a DA.*

*The next step is a sanding block with the pins removed equipped with 36 grit paper.*

*And now we do another test fit and assessment of the tank's progress so far.*

When you've got a rounded shape like this, especially one that's in rough condition, it can take a number of applications to get a nice surface.

Here you can see a low spot that will have to be filled, and the X-pattern left in the mud from our block sanding.

One more application, (number 4) a light one to fill the low spot noted earlier and raise the surface of the tank at the front.

Again, I use a combination of DA, followed by block sanding, both with 36 grit paper, all done before the mud is totally hard.

At this point I'm applying another two coats of primer, I've already applied 3 coats and block sanded with 150 grit.

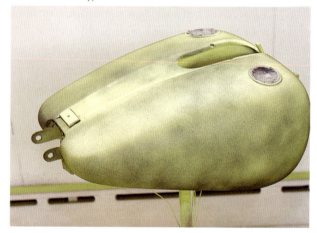

Then comes the guide coat before we start the next round of block sanding.

Now I'm going to work with the DA and a 36 grit pad (not shown), I like to use aggressive grits for sanding mud. Next I go to the sanding pad. Tanks are hard to do, there's so much shape, and this one is in rough condition. Note the picture with the finger pointing out the low spot on the left side, visible because of the different color, note also the X-pattern visible in the mud.

We need one more application of mud. It's important to clean off the plastic mixing pad in-between each batch of filler. We are getting close now so I work with the DA and a 36 grit pad, using it carefully so I don't take off too much material. I'm working the mud while it's only half hard again. Another nice thing about working the mud while it's soft is that the DA won't dig into the old mud, you're only working the new filler.

When the filler is half hard, that's a good time to block. When using the DA you can't get into a pattern, the use must be random or it will show later. Now we blow it off and we're there, except for one little spot that needs spot putty.

## READY FOR PRIMER

The filler is sanded down to the point where there are a few bare metal spots showing, which means there's no more filler on here than there needs to be. The final sanding is 80 grit prior to application of the primer.

The primer being used here is KP 2 CF, mixed 1:1. I have about eight hours of body work invested at this point. I apply three coats of primer, with a SATA HVLP primer gun running at 50 psi.

Before sanding the primer I put on a guide coat, then start the sanding with 150 grit paper on a sanding block (not shown). Then I put on a couple of more coats of primer and another guide coat. These additional steps would be unnecessary if this were a more "normal" tank without so much old body work.

## WET SANDING

The paper I use here is 400, folded per the photos. It's a good idea to soak the paper in water for 20 minutes to soften the backing, it makes the sandpaper work better. You can't use the block on the very curved sections on the bottom for example. The low spots should come out with sanding but if the low area exceeds 1/8 inch in depth, use

*For this next series of block sanding I'm using a flexible pad wrapped in 400 grit paper.*

*It' important to keep the paper wet as I work.*

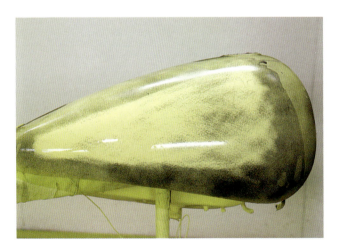

*Part way through the sanding you can see there are some low spots left. Our goal of course is to eliminate all of these.*

As we continue working the tank until most of the guide coat is sanded off...

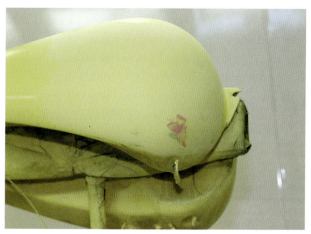

The mixed putty is applied with a small flexible pad and sanded with 400 before it's fully set up.

...except for this little spot on the lower right hand corner...

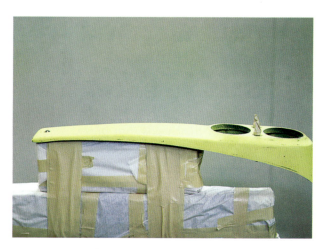

To paint the tank I make a simple little fixture, which is placed near the tank for painting.

...which calls for spot putty mixed on a clean sheet of plastic.

The last thing I do before applying the sealer is tack off the tank.

regular filler. For low areas shallower than that you can use spot putty. Note how the low spots show up at first and then are sanded out.

Unless you use a sanding block you don't know when to quit sanding. On the right front upper corner I've broken through the primer, but that's OK because we are using a catalyzed sealer. But on the lower right corner there's a little nick just above another sand-through spot and we will have to fill that with glaze

As we've done before, I mix the two-part glazing putty until it's a uniform color, apply it to the metal and then you can sand it almost immediately. The sanding is done with 400, the same grit that I was using around that spot. It's such a minor spot we are not going to re-prime, if it were bigger I would re-prime and bake that section. By baking the area we could still paint that same day. Now I'm going to flip the tank and sand the bottom.

I sand inside the tunnel and under the dash just so the paint will stick to those areas. When I paint the tank I will have the dash nearby so they both get painted at the same time with the same number of coats and the same gun. On the dash I sand just until the guide coat is gone, that way I don't sand through the primer.

## APPLY THE SEALER AND BASECOAT

We're using KS 11 for the sealer, mixed 4:1:1. I normally recommend KU 150 catalyst, but if you're painting small objects use the 100, its faster and it's cheaper too. RU 310 is the reducer I'm using. There is no incubation time with this catalyzed acrylic urethane sealer, mix and go. You have to be careful with the catalyst, which is most dangerous when you're pouring it or it's sitting on the bench un-mixed. Always clean the threads on the catalyst can before putting the cap back on.

At this point I go over all the parts with post-sanding cleaner KC 20 and then I do an air and tack. I put on two coats of the sealer with time to allow it to flash between coats. The temperature in our booth is 70 degrees, this is what we consider to be the minimum temperature to paint. Even a few degrees cooler makes a massive difference. When I use the KU 100 I like to re-coat one hour later, the book says up to 24 hours but I like to do it in one. The basecoat we're using here is black diamond

*For a sealer I'm using two coats of black KS 11, with time to allow the paint to flash between coats.*

*Next comes the metallic basecoat black diamond, MBC 03, applied in 3 coats.*

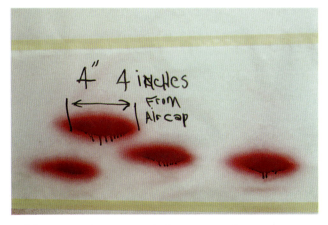

*I like to test the pattern before I start the spraying. For motorcycles the pattern should be 4 inches wide 4 inches from the aircap, though for basecoats the width of the pattern is not as critical.*

Application of the kandy brandywine is next.

We put on a total of 6 coats of kandy, followed by 2 coats of clear.

When the paint no longer strings up onto your finger...

Once the clear is fully cured I scuff the surface with 500 grit paper wet, with a little Ivory liquid in the water so you get a bit of lubricity.

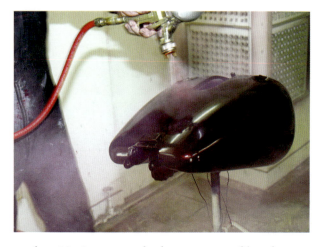

...then it's time to apply the next coat of kandy.

Where there's a small run I use the run file, think of it as a tiny sanding block. It removes the run without removing adjacent paint.

MBC 03. It's a 2:1 mix, with RU 310 reducer. This is basecoat so there is no catalyst. Because of the metallics I don't know if it will go through the strainer. This new material stays in suspension better than other metallics, the particles are lighter and resemble a flake without the work.

I'm using the same DeVilbiss gun we used before. I let the paint flash between coats of the base with a ten minute wait between the last coat of base and the first coat of kandy. I mix the kandy 2:1:1. For motorcycles I like to use the fast reducer, up to about 80 or 85 degrees with extra reduction (one or two ounces per quart) in the first coats.

### KANDY BRANDYWINE.

You have to test the gun pattern before applying the kandy (page 105). I want a four inch pattern four inches from the gun. I do this with the air horns set 90 degrees to their normal position. The first pattern is a bit uneven so I adjust and do another test pattern The fan control is always set all the way out. As I explained in Chapter Three, the pattern is set with the material knob.

When I come out of the booth to get more paint for the gun I always drop the paint that's still in the gun, into the paint I'm going to add to the gun. I mix the two and then re-fill the cup from the mixed paint.

The kandy coats go on quick. Before applying the next coat the paint should be sticky but not string up onto your finger. The metallics used in the MBC paints are classified as a size 90. The range runs from 30 to 150 so these are in the middle.

In this case I put on a total of six coats of kandy. The instructions say five to six. The pressure at the wall is 35 psi with the trigger pulled. This material comes out a tiny bit rough so I apply two coats of clear, UC 35, at the end. I'm using RU 310 reducer and KU 100 catalyst for the clear.

In situations like this the base coat should be darker than the flake so you have the illusion of full coverage. Otherwise the end result looks like dirt.

### READY FOR ART

I baked the parts last night to be sure they're dry this morning. You can use heat lights to expedite the drying time. The light I use is from Hurkules which allows you to bring the lights and

*The first part of laying out the artwork is to find the center of the tank.*

*As I've said before, I like to design right on the tank, here I'm using my thumb to push the tape down...*

*...while I position the tape with my other hand, all the time keeping just a little tension on the tape.*

*Here it's easier to see how I pull the tape around in an arc.*

*It's all a matter of coordination between my left hand and right thumb.*

*A good design should flow. If it doesn't look right I pull the tape up and do that section again.*

heat on gradually so there is no danger of "skinning" the part.

I sand the clear with 500 grit, a lot of custom painters say it's too coarse but that's what I've used all my life. You wouldn't want to go finer than 600.

On the front of the tank there's a little run, so I use a "run file" until I can't feel the run anymore (page 106). You have to be sure to sand the scratches from the run file out with the 500 grit paper. "When you start to see color in the water, it means you've broken through the clear. I get really nervous when that happens. You have to do the bottom too, and unless you flip it over you can't really see what you're doing.

On the dash it's easier to finesse the sanding with your fingers. The shape makes this hard to do. On any peaks or edges you have to lighten up with the sand paper and keep your eyes peeled for any color in the water, if you're not paying attention to what you're doing you can ruin the whole thing. My advice is to take the pressure off the paper anytime you're on an edge.

## THE FIRST LAYOUT

In order to have continuity I'm going to do the last layout first, I don't draw my designs out ahead of time, My goal is to design with the tape. But first I have to find the middle. The tape is crepe tape, 3M masking tape, UPC 06343 1/8th inch. The problem you see with crepe tape, the paint tends to creep under the tape, with our Shimrin base coats the creep is not a problem, I like the masking tape because it turns nice and it tears easy.

Tanks are asymmetrical, you have to find the center and run a piece of tape from front to back. Then I start working on the layout. If the pattern doesn't look right at any time you can pick up the tape and move it. At the top of the tank I try to get the spacing of the ends even because you can see those when you're siting on the bike. I always measure off the dash or the gas openings.

I can eye-ball it faster than I can make a template and use it on the other side. It comes from years of practice, for me it's about speed. It's OK to check one side against the other with the small measuring tape. In this case though the dash is hand made, so I trust my eye as to what looks right.

Your hands need to be super clean for this so no oils are transferred to the tank.

Though you have to be careful that there isn't too much tension on the tape, especially in the corners...

What I like about this crepe tape is the fact that you can just break it off under your thumbnail and start back the other way.

...or it will pop loose when the paint is applied.

This 1/8th inch tape is nice because it turns fairly easily.

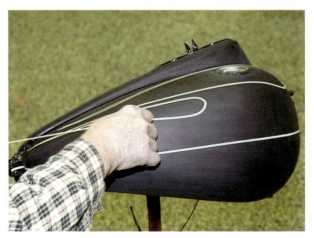

It takes practice to be able to create nice tight, smooth curves like this one.

*My goal here is to squeeze in one more lick on the bottom of the tank.*

*Which requires another very tight turn.*

The flames have to sweep, this is critical. And both sides have to be the same. Like I said, that old adage about only being able to see one side at a time is a cop out. You have to get the first side right and then check the second side against the first.

Do the taping in layers, so it all comes off in one pull. Sometimes we use 3/4 inch tape and sometimes 1/4 inch, it depends on the situation. You can also use an X-acto knife to cut the tape at the curve. When I mask off the rest of the tank I try and hit 50% of the outline tape (note the photo on the bottom left of page 111).

I put the tape on back to front, so when you pick up the front of the tape the whole area will peel off. On the tight corners it's easier to use 1/4 inch tape, it will turn tight where the 3/4 inch won't.

You have to relax the tape into the turn, otherwise the fresh paint will cause it to release. On the really tight turns it's better to cut the tape, because if you make it turn too tight it might be so tight that it will release later. You have to watch for mistapes and spots where the tape doesn't quite cover or where it's starting to pull away from the metal.

**FENDER LAYOUTS**

On the front fender I ran a center line with tape first, then I did the layout. Before doing the layout for the rear fender I put the struts in place and then ran a center line. You don't want the strut

*And a short run toward the back of the tank.*

*Now I'm going to run the tape up to the front of the tank and create another lick.*

*The wider tape is hard to turn, it's usually easier to just cut it neatly with a razor or X-acto knife.*

*Here you can see what I've created. I call these scallop-style flames. The length will help give the bike a sense of motion.*

*I'm using the same technique for laying down the wide tape that I used for the 1/8th inch crepe tape.*

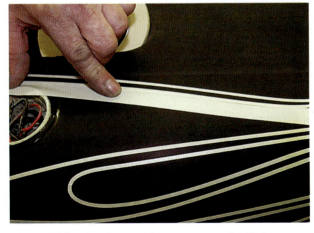

*Once I like the design it's time to mask off the rest of the tank. The wider tape should cover half (50%) of the 1/8th in tape.*

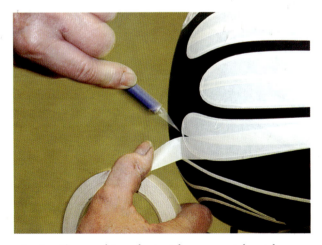

*Again, I'm masking the inside areas with wider tape that I cut neatly with the X-acto knife.*

*You can also use 1/4 inch tape, which will turn, to make off the inside of the curves.*

*I'm using my thumb again to guide the tape, and being careful to lay it down without any tension.*

to cut off the flame or the layout will look like an after thought.

## KAMELEON KOLORS

I apply three coats of the color-change paint with the DeVilbiss HVLP detail gun. The new Kameleon materials are unique, you wouldn't think it would go with what we're doing, but it will be spectacular. I'm using copper red-to-green for most of the flame. Then I fade in some green-to-blue for the front and at the ends of the licks.

I recommend you always stir the SG 100 before use because the two resins can separate. I start with two cups of SG and 2 cups of 310 for 100% reduction. I stir it all together then pour some off to mix the Kameleon kolors. For the blue to green I start with three ounces of mixed SG 100 and add 1/2 teaspoon of powder. For the copper red-to-green I start with 1 heaping teaspoon in the nine ounces, but that doesn't look like enough so I add another 1/2 teaspoon.

After straining it into the cup we put on three coats of the copper red-to-green, in quick succession, adding the next coat once the previous coat is no longer sticky. Then I fog in some green-to-blue at the ends of the flames and in the area at the front of the licks. To protect the paint we just sprayed I do one coat of SG 100 at 100% reduction over the whole thing. Because of the final SG we can use a scotch brite pad to clean up any areas where the paint crept under

You might think the hard part is done once the layout is finished, but the masking is just as much work.

The Kameleon paint comes as a dry powder and needs to be mixed with SG 100.

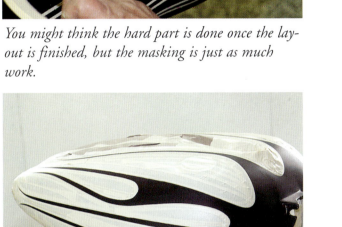

I take time to look over the tank once the masking is finished. This is our last chance to change anything about the design we don't like.

I start off with a heaping teaspoon in 9 ounces of mixed SG 100.

It's important, and sometimes difficult, to transfer the layout used on the tank to the fenders.

You have to trust your eye. After mixing in one teaspoon, I look at the mix under a small spot light and decide to add more Kameleon.

*The copper red-to-green goes on in three quick coats...*

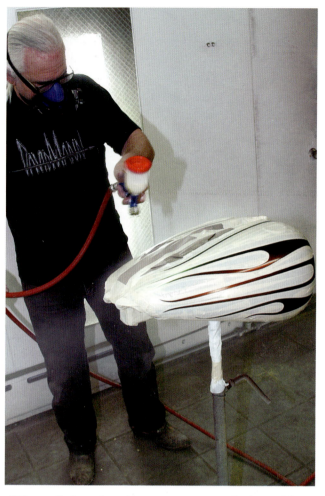

*...then I add green-to-blue highlights at the front of the tank and at the ends.*

*When all the color-change paint is applied, I add one coat of SG 100.*

*Now we can pull the tape, which comes off easily in one or two big pieces because of the way we laid it down. It's always better to pull the tape sooner, rather than later, to minimize pulling up any paint.*

the tape. The pad gets rid of any little pieces of tape or over-spray. Then I rinse the tank with water and blow it dry. This way I don't need to use a tack rag or touch any of the parts. This step is critical because anything that's stuck on here now will be buried in clear.

After the tank is free of masking tape we re-tape just the two gas tank openings and apply the clear, UC 35. The clear goes on in three coats, a quick bond coat to help adhesion of the coats to follow, then two wet coats. The bond coat is really just a medium coat applied fast. The clear is mixed to the standard ratio of 2:1:1, with RU 310 and KU 100. Remember, if there's a U in the paint code, it requires a catalyst. The exception is the striping paint, if it's going to be cleared then you don't need the catalyst.

Note, the original plan was to pinstripe the first set of flames but not the second. Later, after looking at the finished job, we decided not to do any pinstriping on the first layout, the tapeouts were sharp, with no creep under the edge of the tape.

The Shimrin bases are great for this, they don't creep under the tape edge. And three medium coats only build 1/2 mil, which is very minimal and easy to smooth out with clearcoats. I rarely do art work with catalyzed paint because of how high the paints build.

*This is a good time to re-tape the two gas tank openings.*

*Next we go over the tank with a gray Scotch-brite pad to clean up any little mis-tapes.*

*I want to layout another compete set of flames, but first I need a good clearcoat to work on. This is UC 35 being applied. I put on one light bond coat, then two wet coats.*

It looks like we're done, but there's another whole layout to follow.

Before starting the next layout I have to scuff the tank with 500 grit paper.

On the fender you can really see the effect of the green-to-blue used at the very front, and the brilliance lent to the whole piece by the new MBC basecoats.

Before starting on the next set of flames I have to find the center of the tank. The hard part is creating a second set of flames that add to the overall design without taking anything away from the first set.

## ONE MORE SET OF FLAMES

On this second layout we are using plastic tape, 3/32 inch "edge" tape from Finesse, so we get a nice clean edge. I don't want to pinstripe the secondary set of flames.

The second color, sapphire blue, is part of the Kameleon II line but has a more subtle color shift than some of the other color-change materials.

I use 500 grit paper wet to scuff the surface with a little Ivory in the water before starting on the next layout. This flexible pad I'm using really helps to flatten things because it concentrates the effort on the high spots. You're never going to eliminate all the shine. When we're done there's a little left along the edges of the flames, but you need to eliminate most of the shine. Keep in mind you only have two coats of clear, you want to be careful not to break through the clear. The color sanding doesn't take long. Sometimes you can tell how well you're doing by feel.

When I start taping I leave a little folded-over tab on each end of the tape so I can pick it up and make a change if I need to. That's what I like about this tape, the adhesive they use allows you to pick it up, move it and put it back down.

To make sure the tape is stuck down I like to run a knife blade over the material, though you can also use a little roller instead. And you can't stretch the tape or it will release once the paint hits.

*I'm using the same basic flame shape for the second set that I used for the first set of flames.*

*For the second set of flames I'm using plastic tape...*

*...so I get a clean tape edge that won't need to be pinstriped. Like the Sportster, when you're doing a second layout, you have to keep track of which design goes on top of the other in all the places they cross.*

*I'm running the new paint licks between the first set.*

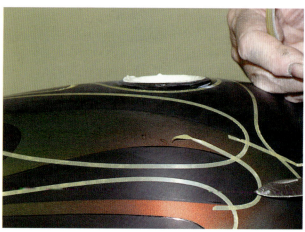

*I like to run a knife blade over the edges of the tape to make sure it's stuck down to the tank.*

*The second set needs to stand apart from the first.*

*Here I'm masking off the area where the two layouts overlap. This second set of flames will run under the first.*

*Though the design looks busy, it will all come together when I'm finished.*

*Quarter inch plastic tape is useful to mask out some of these areas where the two layouts cross.*

During the second layout I have to tape over the places where the second design runs "under" the first.

Once I have the design laid out it's time to mask out all the areas where we don't want tape. I use 1/4 inch tape where I have to and then switch to the 3/4 inch tape as soon as I can. For bigger areas I use paper, because paper is cheaper than tape. With the 3/4 inch tape I try not to turn it, it wrinkles too much, I tear it and reapply in the curves to avoid the wrinkles.

Our basecoats are not catalyzed, so you can wipe off any mistakes. The saphirre blue goes on in three medium coats, then a little green-to-blue for highlights (page 120). I mix it to get coverage the first time.

For the green-to-blue, the gun is adjusted to a dot pattern, with 20 psi of pressure, I spray just the ends of the licks and a dot in the middle.

Then I put on one coat of SG 100 right away. Now it's time to pull the tape and do the clear. It's kind of funny, we spent all day on this to get ready for 15 minutes of paint.

The clearcoat we use now is UC 35, and I put it on in three coats, one light and two wet. The UFC 35 goes on last.

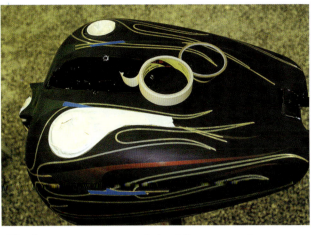

*The layout wraps around the filler cap, so I start my making there.*

*Plastic tape is a good product to use where one lick crosses another because the paint is less likely to creep.*

*Again, this is the last time we have an opportunity to change the shape of the flame licks.*

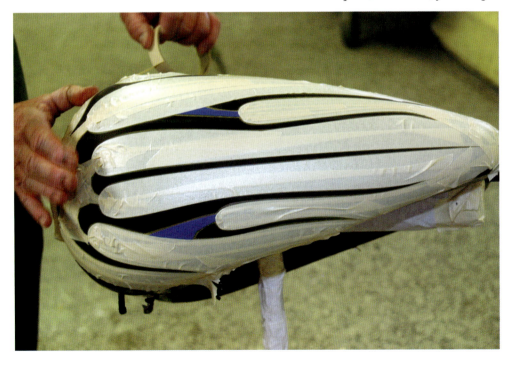

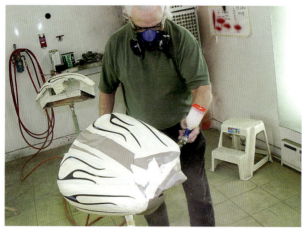

The primary color I'm using for the second set of flames is sapphire blue.

The gun is adjusted to a dot pattern first...

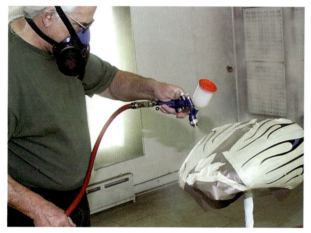

The DeVilbiss HVLP gun is the same one I used for the other set of flames. You don't need a big gun for this type of work.

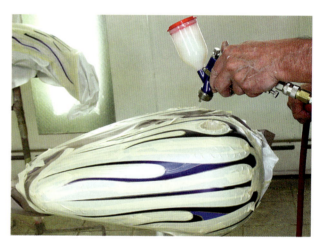

then I highlight the ends of the flames...

For highlights I mix up some green-to-blue. I mix it strong enough to cover in only one coat.

...the bowl, and a spot in the middle of each lick. The last paint to go on before pulling tape is a quick coat of SG 100 clear.

## OUT OF THE PAINT BOOTH

After pulling the tape and applying three coats of UC 35 clear, we take the parts out into the sun to let the customer gauge the paint job. "Absolutely radiant" is how Shantha describes the finished job. After a little discussion we decided to use the job as it came out of the paint booth, without any pin-stripes. As Shantha explained, "it's perfect the way it is." And the tape lines are so clean that you don't need a pinstripe to hide any flaws or mis-tapes.

---

### Undercoat the Fenders

I like to undercoat the bottoms of the fend-ers (not shown) with 2 coats of bedliner, or rubberized undercoating. Any rocks that come up sound less tinny, but it's more so rocks won't create a star pattern if they hit the bottom of the fender. And it makes the finished fender look really neat.

---

## COLOR SANDING THE SHEET METAL

I'm using the flat-sanding DA (page 122), it has no "rocker" or wobble to the pad like a more typical DA has. These are 800 grit pads from 3M, they Velcro on to the pad. I have the speed turned down pretty low. I stay away from edges and cor-ners, because even with 800 grit it removes the paint fast, that's what you want but it's easy to sand through. This paper is available all the way to 2000 grit.

You have to watch for colored dust, just like you watch for colored water, it means you've gone through the clearcoat into the color. So I will do those areas later with wet sanding. With this process you sand and then wipe the dust off. It's better and faster than wet sanding because you can see what you're doing. You sand, then wipe it off. We are blocking as well as sanding. Along the way you will find little low spots and some high spots caused by dust nibs. Occasionally you have to take a Scotch-brite pad and wipe the dust off the sand-ing pad. What we're looking for here, after we wipe it off, is no shiny spots.

We follow a pattern here: sand a little, stop, wipe the pad and the part, then check your work. I'm concentrating on what I'm doing, the color of

*I don't wait very long before pulling the tape. Then we check for mis-tapes, scuff the tank and apply 3 coats of clear.*

*Now you can see how the two layouts work together. You have to be able to see all this in your head (or on a sketch) ahead of time.*

*The use of the metallic basecoat under the Kameleon makes for super bright flame licks. The sapphire is designed to have a fairly subtle color shift.*

For the color sanding we're using the flat sanding orbital sander equipped with 800 grit pads.

Near the end of the sheet metal sequence we take a break to finish the chassis parts. To paint round parts I like to adjust the gun to a dot pattern.

I'm sanding with low pressure and the sander speed set pretty low.

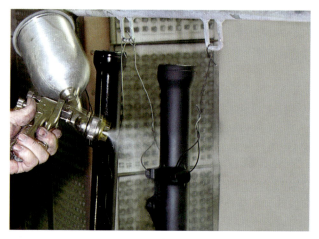

The sequence of painting chassis parts is very much the same as that used on the sheet metal, with a few changes as noted in the text.

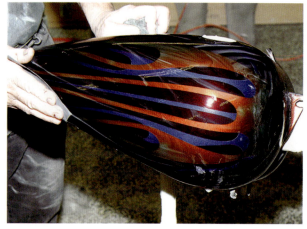

Wet sanding with 500 grit wet is the last step before application of the final clearcoats.

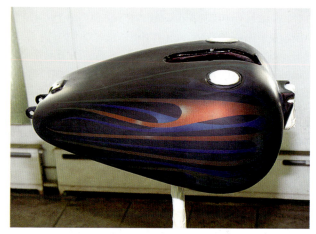

Back to the sheet metal, the tank is flattened and tacked and ready for the final clear. We've decided not to pinstripe any of the flames.

the dust should be white. This process is fast, the results are immediate.

This flattened it, it's like a power block. So now all I have to do is wet sand with 500 grit wet. This is the final touch. Wet sanding cleans out all the dust, and gives it a little more bite for the clearcoat. Things get done faster and they're better that way.

## Paint the Chassis Parts

Like the sheet metal parts, all the chassis parts have been media blasted to the bare substrate. For primer you can use one coat of KP 2 CF and wait two hours and then paint them. Or apply two coats, let them sit overnight, lightly sand with 500, and then spray them. I decide on two coats because the additional coat of primer will fill little low spots or any pattern left by the media blasting.

If you keep your hands off the parts you don't transfer any oils so you don't need a chemical wash down. I like to just wash the parts with hot water then blow them dry with compressed air. Then tack them and you're ready to paint. We tape off any close tolerances areas, like inside the triple trees and where the axle goes through the lower legs. And anywhere there are threads.

The sealer I'm using is the same sealer we used on the sheet metal parts, black, KS 11, mixed 4:1:1 and applied in one coat. The black diamond, MBC 03, is mixed next, to a ratio of 2:1 without any catalyst. We put on a total of three coats, I shoot the first coat, then the second and third as soon as the previous coat is dry to the touch, which takes about five minutes in a 70 degree booth. By the time I have the kandy mixed the parts will be dry enough to shoot.

The kandy koncentrate, KK 01, is good for areas that are not required to be light-fast, for big areas that are exposed to the sun it is not advised. As we mentioned before, the KK materials are mixed 8:1 with SG 100. For this next step I apply four coats, using a restricted trigger pull, with the air nozzle three to four inches from the gun. We don't want to blow a lot of paint in the air.

AX 01 accelerator is added to reduce between-coat times. Less reducer in this mix. I'm applying four coats of the kandy mix.

The clear I'm using here is UC 35. 35 stands

*For the final clear I'm using UFC 35, 3 coats total including the bond coat. We are shooting with 40 psi at the regulator, slightly less at the gun.*

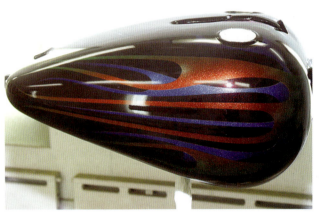

*I put the last two coats on super wet and this is the result. All that's left is one more round of sanding and polishing.*

*I start with the flat sanding orbital sander and some 1500 dry (not shown) and move to the Dynabrade connected to a pail of water.*

*For the Dynabrade I use 2000 and then 4000 grit pads with water.*

*The next step is compound and a cut-wool pad on a big buffer.*

*When it comes to compound and glaze, there are a number of good products, including Meguiar's and Wizards.*

for 3.5 VOC, government rules. The mixing ratio is 2:1:1, with 310 reducer and no accelerator but I will reduce the amount of reducer slightly because I want this to be a little bit thicker. After all, it's got to take the stones and gravel from the road. I apply two coats with a five to eight minute wait between coats. The last coat will be super wet.

## SHEET METAL PARTS, THE FINAL CLEAR

At this point we have all the sheet metal parts moved into the booth and we've wet down the floor. We are using UFC 35 mixed 2:1:1-1/2, using more reducer because these are flow coats. This is the higher gloss clear that's easier polishing. Again, I start with one bond coat and follow that with two super wet coats. We want these to be super smooth flow coats. I have a six inch pattern six inches from the gun with 50% overlap. It doesn't hurt to add a tiny bit of extra catalyst, because when you add the reducer it slows the cure, the extra (1 oz to a quart) will quicken the set up time.

With the paint bag in the cup, the paint is under a vacuum so you can paint upside down and you never get a drip from the gun. I'm using 40 psi at the regulator, probably 30 or 32 at the gun. This UFC clear is great, it goes on like glass.

## FINAL SAND AND BUFF ON THE TANK.

The process used here to produce a very bright sooth shine is pretty much the same that we've used in the earlier chapters. The first step is to sand the surface flat with the Mirka Bulldog and a 1500 grit dry pad. The wet sanding starts with the small "wet" Dynabrade sander. This sander just vibrates, it doesn't actually orbit. We start with a 2000 grit pad on the Dynabrade, then switch to a 4000 grit pad. All these pads attach in hook-and-loop fashion.

After I've finished with the sanders it's time for buffing. Our first step is Perfect-It III rubbing compound from 3M and a cut-wool pad on a big variable speed buffer, which I run at 1500 rpm.

Next we apply the Perfect-It III machine glaze, number 05937. For both the compound and the glaze the buffer speed should be in the 1500 to 1800 rpm range. For this glaze we're using a foam pad instead of the cut-wood pad we used with the compound. I use less of the glaze than the rubbing compound. The only thing left is the application of some Kosmic Shine.

*There are a variety of products that can be applied by hand as the final step...*

*...I'm using the Kosmic Shine from House of Kolor.*

*In the end the finished paint job is very bright, especially when the sun comes out. Not only is this a unique paint job, it's a paint job that changes with the light and with the angle of view. The best thing about the powdered Kameleons is the fact that they don't bronze and they can be added to other colors for unique effects.*

# Chapter Seven

# Kandy Koated Mustang

## Kandy Paint on the top *and* the bottom

The 1967 Mustang shown here is a personal project of mine. This fastback is a car I've been working on for well over a year now. I had the body stripped with plastic media to remove the paint and then dipped to remove the rust.

We've started this painting sequence at a point where the body is almost ready for final primer. Because we covered the body work part of the Camaro project so thoroughly, we've decided to start this project at a point where most of the

*We only found a little rust when we pulled the Mustang apart and had it stripped to bare metal. Even without too much rust though, the restoration turned out to be a lot of work.*

body work is already finished.

The primer we're using here is the KP 2 CF. We've worked hard to get the primer into all the cracks and crevices of the body shell and chassis. I don't want any bare metal anywhere on this car. Once we get the car on the rotisserie we will be able to make sure the bottom is primered as thoroughly as everything else.

## Block Sanding

The first round of body work and sanding is already done, this is intermediary sanding. And to check our work I put a guide coat on the car before we start the block sanding. As I've said again and again, the shape of the block must match the shape of the panel or recess.

The idea is to use the sanding block in an X-pattern so you don't create any ridges or low spots. When you're done with the sanding the guide coat should all be gone, it if isn't there are remaining low spots. We are using the big block from Adjustable Flexibility Sanders, with 80 grit sanding paper, for this part of the sequence.

These big blocks really do the job. With the rods out they will follow the contour of the quarter panel, with the rods in they do a good job on a flat panel. I never had these blocks before, they're really handy.

As I work closer and closer to the fender well I go

*We took the Mustang apart until there weren't any parts left to take off the body shell. then everything went to Kirby's to be stripped.*

*At this point the first round of body work is done, most of the parts and the inner body shell are coated in primer.*

127

We are getting close to the final body work and primer, so I've put a guide coat on everything.

The shape of the block is determined by the shape of the body panel.

A long block with the pins in place is a good tool for big nearly flat areas like this quarter panel.

The long blocks are very useful, but to finish the dished upper quarter panel we're going to need a block with a radius that matches the shape of the metal.

to the smaller block with no rods. This is my last chance to use putty. When the car goes into final prime I'd like to say that's it. For some of these areas I'm going to need a block with a tight radius.

A lot of the primer you put on the car is going to come off. Think how much longer it would take to fix this if I used finer paper. In fact, we're probably spending more time than necessary but we want it really nice. The preparation is the key to the whole job.

As I get into the lower part of the quarter panel I go to a smaller and smaller block, most of these are flexible too, that's very important. The thing you have to avoid is pattern sanding. For the area right around the fender lip I use the round block. When I'm all through I will take a three-fold piece of sanding paper and go over all those areas by hand.

Any place there's a dark area, that's the guide coat that hasn't been removed. My goal is to be sure all those areas are eliminated. I do the peak of the fender with a small block and almost no pressure. You have to be extra careful with the sanding anytime there's an edge.

There are a couple of small pinholes in the quarter panel up near the top and I found another little low spot just behind

*With the rods in place the long block works well on the lower quarter panel.*

*A small flexible block with a small radius is the best way to finish the lip at the fender well.*

129

I finish the fender lip by hand, sometimes the best sanding block is no block at all.

Spot putty is a good choice for small low spots like this one.

I like to apply the spot putty right after I mix it, with a small flexible pad.

Before the putty is fully formed I go after it with a round sanding block and 80 grit paper. Then all it will need is a little finish work done by hand.

*After cleaning the car, areas where I have filler or putty get primered first. Then I start applying primer to the rest of the car.*

the driver's door opening. For those small areas I will use Evercoat spot-lite putty. This stuff sets up really quick and if you get on it when it's still soft it sands really nice. You have to be careful of using too much spot putty on too big an area though, because it's actually harder to sand than the regular two-part plastic filler.

Sometimes I work the puttied area with coarse paper and then finish with something finer. Other times you need to guide coat over the putty and block sand the area to be

*I'm as careful in applying primer as I am when shooting kandy and always use straight line painting techniques.*

*We are put at least 3 coats of primer on the car, areas where we did body work get 2 additional coats.*

*I'm painting with 50% overlap between passes, walking the full length of the quarter panel.*

*Getting the car on the rotisserie is a lot of work, but once it's bolted on you have access to the bottom that can't be obtained by other way. P. Kosmoski*

*With wheels on one end and caster plates on the other it's fairly easy to roll the whole thing into the booth. P. Kosmoski*

*We spent a tremendous amount of time repairing small holes in the floor and detailing the bottom. Now we can do a quality paint job.*

*The first step is cleaning followed by air and tack.*

*The long center pole is always in the way, sometimes I adjust the gun to a dot pattern and shoot across to the other side of the chassis.*

sure there aren't any remaining high or low spots.

## MORE PRIMER

Now it's time to blow off the car and wipe it down before applying primer. The primer must be mixed ahead of time, it needs an incubation period, and that's already been done. The nice thing about this is you can put the primer in the 'fridge after it's mixed and it won't get hard. So if you mix too much material you can save it that way.

Just like we did with the Camaro, I wipe down the car, using two rags, one to wipe the clearer on and the other to wipe it off. You never want to put on more than you can wipe off before it dries.

I start the application of primer on the areas where we put the spot putty. Then I go back and primer the entire car. This is the first of three total coats we will put on the car at this time. The air pressure during primer application is 55 pounds at the regulator. We are using a dedicated primer gun, a Sata HVLP.

## THE ROTISSERIE

By mounting the car on our hand-built rotisserie we're able to tilt the car first one way, so I can do the bottom of the passenger side, then the other way so I can paint the driver's side. It's important to get the paint into all the recesses. Some times I adjust the gun to a straight dot pattern and shoot the paint across to the inside of the frame rails on the other side.

*You have to work with the gun to be sure and get primer into all the little cracks and crevices.*

*To paint the inside of the right frame rail you have to reach over the bar and shoot across the car with the gun adjusted to a dot pattern again.*

*After putting on 2 coats of solar gold you can see why I wanted to use the yellow primer as the sealer coat.*

*Like the primer and the base, the kandy is hard to apply because of the convoluted shapes.*

*It can be hard to get really nice kandy coverage of a shape like this, but luckily no one is going to go over it with a magnifying glass when it's finished.*

*Despite the shape and all the lumps and bumps I try to keep the gun-to-surface distance constant at 6 inches, and the gun moving in a straight line.*

The rotisserie makes it so much easier to do a really nice job of painting the bottom of the car. This way we can paint both the top and bottom of this car with the same paint. Who says you can't kandy paint the bottom?

## PAINTING THE MUSTANG'S BOTTOM.

I'm using our KP 2 CF primer again, but this time with 20% over reduction. When it's over reduced it will work on bare metal as a sealer. It's got the color I want, that's the big thing. No one makes a yellow sealer. I don't want to dirty a pressure pot with this stuff, it's hard to clean. So I will do the best I can with a standard gun adjusted to 45 psi at the gun.

For our basecoat we are using BC 01 solar gold. This is one of our Shimrin basecoats. These non-catalyzed paints go on fast and dry fast. For the kandy topcoat I've decided to use UK 8 kandy tangerine. I will probably put on four or five coats. Sometimes I just shoot it 'til I like it.

I'm using a new HVLP pressure pot from DeVilbiss for the ease of application, equipped with a small 1.1 nozzle-needle combination. The pressure pot can affect the finish of kandy paint and we are testing to see if the new pressure pot with a small orifice will help give us a nice finish. I have five lbs. of pressure on the paint and 40 at the regulator.

*Painting the chassis is a lot of work, partly because of all the extra masking. P. Kosmoski*

*This is what the bottom looks like after four coats of kandy.*

*After the kandy is dry we mask off the big openings in the chassis before painting the engine compartment and inside of the body. Note how the paint became darker*

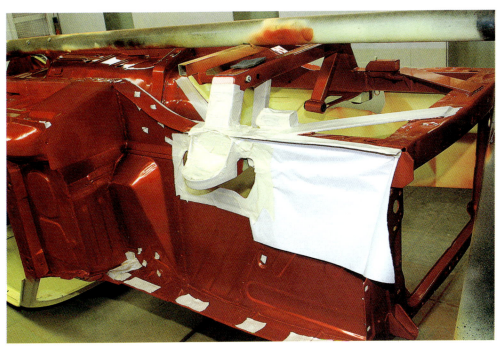

*Each step of this paint job involves a lot of work. Here we had to mask off the rest of the body...*

*...before painting the inner shell, and then the dash in a separate, additional, operation.*

*Kandy tangerine applied over our solar gold creates a nice rich color that I've always liked, and one that should look good on this Mustang.*

*When the black is dry and the masking paper is removed, we can re-install the doors, trunk and hood. After doing a little last minute body work we can reverse the masking seen earlier, replacing the paper on the outside of the body with paper and tape on the inside.*

For the bottom of the car I ended up putting on two coats of base and four coats of kandy. Then I had some kandy left so I mixed that with clear and put on two coats of tinted clear for a total of 8 coats. It's a lot of work to paint the bottom, partly because you're lugging around the pressure pot. And it's hard to work around that center bar as you paint the bottom.

Once the bottom is finished we have to tape off all the openings in the chassis so we don't get any over spray on the new kandy paint. The body shell is totally stripped and primered. Now is the time to paint all those inner surfaces, the engine compartment and even the dashboard. For painting inside the shell I use UB 4 jet set black without any clearcoat. For the dash though we took another step. First we color sanded the UB 4, then applied another coat of UB 4 mixed 50:50 with UC 35 clear to create a flow coat that leaves a really nice surface behind.

## A SMALL SETBACK

At this point I thought all the body work was done, that we were ready to start painting the body. When we hung the doors in place though I quickly discovered that the fit between the door and the body was pretty poor. This means that after hanging all the sheet metal on the car we had to do more body work (not shown) to make sure all the panels line up correctly.

*When we taped out the opening we left a tab that the masking paper could be taped to, this makes masking out so much easier.*

*The basecoat is applied following the same pattern established during application of the primer. I start with a pressure pot but switched to a conventional gun for the rest of the coats.*

137

*This is the first coat of solar gold being applied to the left side of the roof...*

*The inner lip of the trunk opening needs to be painted in a separate operation.*

*...followed by the other side of the roof...*

*I have to walk the long sides of the car, being careful to keep the gun moving at a constant speed...*

*...the rear roof pillar, the top of the quarter panel and then the right side of the trunk.*

*...while maintaining a consistent gun to sheet metal distance.*

With the black fully dried and all the sheet metal in place we carefully tape the areas around the doors. The idea is to leave a tab sticking out that we can tape to when it's time to paint the rest of the body. That way we don't have to tape from the back side first.

## APPLY SEALER AND FINAL PAINT

Though it took a little longer than I planned, we finally have all the panels aligned and the body ready for primer. As I said before, the sealer I'm using is KP 2 CF primer over reduced 20% with EP 3. I put on two coats of the sealer before moving on to the basecoat.

To get nice even coverage I put on three coats of the solar gold basecoat. The first coat is applied with the pressure pot with eight pounds of pressure on the pot and 40 pounds of pressure at the regulator. But the finish looks a little streaky so I change to a conventional HVLP gun (a DeVilbiss GT-1) for coats number two and three. As always I have to let each coat flash before the next application goes on, and before application of the kandy.

The UK 8 Kandy Tangerine is mixed 2:1:1 with an extra ounce and a half of reducer per mixed quart. Never mix more than a gallon of material at a time, it will set up if it sits too long. I had a guy call me one time, he'd mixed up three

*The pressure pot means you won't run out of paint, but it's a lot more weight to lug around the booth.*

*After painting the right side I finish the driver's side of the hood...*

*...then it's back to walking the car, on the left side this time. The paint suit is an important part of any painter's tool kit. It keeps the paint off your clothes and body, but just as important, it keeps lint on your clothes from becoming airborne and contaminating the fresh paint. The hot spot on the quarter panel is a reflection from one of the booth lights.*

For the solar gold basecoat I put on a total of 3 coats. This gives me nice color and coverage.

...were just practice sessions for the kandy application. By now I'm an expert at painting this particular body.

A kandy paint job is one of those things that separates the men from the buys. Your technique and gun set up need to be just right.

Everything that's been said about consistent speed and distance, and moving like a robot, counts double during the kandy application.

The pattern I follow is the same one I've been using throughout all the steps in this paint job. All those primer and basecoat applications...

In this case I've left the right side of the car for last.

gallons of paint well before starting the paint job. By the time he got to the end it had turned to Jell-O. He was mad as hell but it wasn't our fault.

You have to start shooting immediately after mixing the paint because the pot life is only three to four hours depending on the temperature and humidity and the reducer you use. The extra reducer provides better atomization and gives you better control.

The window for application of the first kandy coat is fifteen minutes to one hour after the last application of basecoat.

The kandy coats go on in quick succession, but it's still a lot of work to put on six coats of paint, keeping the gun speed and gun-to-car distance consistent all the way through.

For application of the kandy I use the DeVilbiss GT-1 gun equipped with a 1.3 mm fluid nozzle running on 30 psi at the gun.

A smart kandy painter thinks on his or her feet making adjustments to the application as required to maintain uniformity. On certain vehicles a varied starting point makes for more uniform coverage. You need to concentrate on the tone of the color.

Though it's not shown, I will follow the same sequence of clearcoat application and color sanding detailed in the Camaro chapter.

*The next coat can go on as soon as the paint doesn't string up on my finger when I touch it.*

*I put on a total of 6 coats of the kandy tangerine, always starting and stopping at the same point.*

*This is what it looks like after 6 coats of kandy. Fluorescent booth lighting does little to show the amazing depth that is created by a good kandy paint job.*

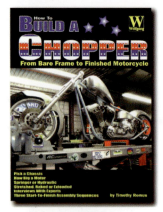

## HOW TO BUILD A CHOPPER

Designed to help you build your own chopper, this book covers History, Frames, Chassis Components, Wheels and Tires, Engine Options, Drivetrains, Wiring, Sheet Metal and Hardware. Included are assembly sequences from the Arlen Ness, Donnie Smith and American Thunder shops. Your best first step! Order today.

Choppers are back! Learn from the best how to build yours.
12 chapters cover:
- Use of Evo, TC, Shovel, Pan or Knucklehead engines
- Frame and running gear choices
- Design decisions - short and stubby or long and radical?
- Four, five or six-speed trannies

| Twelve Chapters | 144 Pages | $24.95 | Over 300 photos-over 50% color |

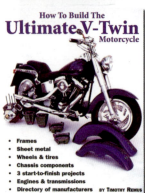

## BUILD THE ULTIMATE V-TWIN MOTORCYCLE

An explosion of new parts from the motorcycle aftermarket now makes it possible to build your own motorcycle from scratch. One designed from the start to answer your need for speed and style. This book is intended to help you make intelligent choices from among the vast number of frames, engines and accessories available today.

You can assemble all those parts into a running motorcycle with tips from men who build bikes professionally. Learn which is the best wiring harness or transmission and the best way to install those parts on your new bike.

After designing, choosing and assembling, all that's left is the registration and insurance. From the first concept to the final bolt, from dream to reality. Yes, you can build your own motorcycle.

| Ten Chapters | 144 Pages | $19.95 | Over 250 photos |

## AMERICAN V-TWIN ENGINE

Everything you need to build or buy the right V-twin motor for your dream ride. Informative text illustrated with more than 300 photos. Covers Evos and Twin Cam.

- TC History
- TC Development
- TC 88-B
- TC Troubles
- TC Hop Up
- TC Cam & Big-Bore install

- Evo Planning
- Evo Carbs
- Evo Cams
- Evo Head & Porting
- Evo Combinations

- Evo Big Block Engines
- Evo Cam Install
- Engine Assembly
- Large Sources section

| Fifteen Chapters | 160 Pages | $21.95 | Over 250 photos |

## HOW TO BUILD A KIT BIKE

How To Build a Kit Bike explains how to choose the best kit and then assemble those parts into a complete running motorcycle. See bikes built in the shops of: Cory Ness, Kendall Johnson and American Thunder. If you own a kit or plan to buy a kit bike, this is the book you need — designed to help you turn that pile of parts into your own very cool motorcycle.

Eight chapters with 300+ photos & illustrations.
- Tools and Fasteners
- Soft-tail, Twin-shock and Hardtail
- 4 Start-to-Finish Assembly Sequences
- Kits From All The Major Manufacturers

| Eight Chapters | 144 Pages | $24.95 | Over 300 photos, 60% color |

# More Great Books From Wolfgang Publications!

## http://www.wolfgangpublications.com

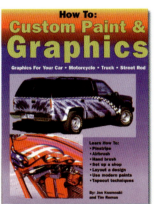

## HOW TO: CUSTOM PAINT & GRAPHICS

A joint effort of the master of custom painting, Jon Kosmoski and Tim Remus, this is the book for anyone who wants to try their hand at dressing up their street rod, truck or motorcycle with lettering, flames or exotic graphics. A great companion to Kustom Painting Secrets (below).

7 chapters include:
• Shop tools and equipment
• Paint and materials
• Letter & pinstripe by hand
• Design and tapeouts
• Airbrushing
• Hands-on, Flames and signs
• Hands-on, Graphics

| Seven Chapters | 144 Pages | $24.95 | Over 250 photos, 50% in color |

## KUSTOM PAINTING SECRETS

More from the master! From the basics to advanced custom painting tricks, Jon Kosmoski shares his 30 years of experience in this book. Photos by publisher Tim Remus bring Jon's text to life. A must for anyone interested in the art of custom painting.

7 chapters include:
• History of House of Kolor
• How to Set up a shop
• Color painting sequences
• Prepare for paint
• Final paint application
• Hands-on, basic paint jobs
• Hands-on, beyond basic paint
• Hands-on, custom painting

| Seven Chapters | 128 Pages | $19.95 | 250 photos with color section |

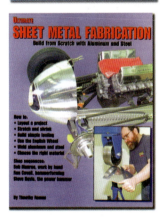

## ULTIMATE SHEET METAL FABRICATION

In an age when most products are made by the thousands, many yearn for the one-of-kind metal creation. Whether you're building or restoring a car, motorcycle, airplane or (you get the idea), you'll find the information you need to custom build your own parts from steel or aluminum.

11 chapters include:
• Layout a project
• Pick the right material
• Shrinkers & stretchers
• English wheel
• Make & use simple tooling
• Weld aluminum or steel
• Use hand and power tools

| Eleven Chapters | 144 Pages | $19.95 | Over 350 photos |

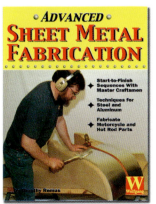

## ADVANCED SHEET METAL FABRICATION

Advanced Sheet Metal Fabrication Techniques, is a photo-intensive how-to book. See Craig Naff build a Rolly Royce fender, Rob Roehl create a motorcycle gas tank, Ron Covell form part of a quarter midget body and Fay Butler shape an aircraft wheel fairing. Methods and tools include English wheel, power hammer, shrinkers and stretchers, and of course the hammer and dolly.

• Sequences in aluminum and steel
• Multi-piece projects
• Start to finish sequences
• From building the buck to shaping the steel
• Includes interviews with the metal shapers
• Automotive, motorcycle and aircraft

| 7 Chapters | 144 Pages | $24.95 | 144 pages, over 300 photos - 60% color |

# Sources

Adjustable Flexibility Sanders
John Wheeler
Order: 877 459 7167
Tech: 651 459 7167
FAX: 651 459 7167
www.adjustflexsand.com

Dayton Reliable Air Filter
2294 N. Moraine Dr.
Dayton, Ohio 45439
1-800-699-0747
Fax: (937) 293-3975
www.reliablefilter.com

DeBeer
(A division of Valspar Refinish)
Spray filler

DeVilbiss
(ITW Automotive Refinishing)
1724 Indian Wood Circle,
Suite J-K
Maumee, OH 43537
419 891 8100
www.devilbiss.com
Tech line: 800 445 3988

Dynabrade Sanders
8989 Sheridan Dr.
Clarence, NY 14031
716 631 0100
www.dynabrade.co

Eastwood Company
Auto body tools and supplies
1-800-343-9353
www.eastwoodco.com

Fibre Glass-Evercoat
Spray filler
6600 Cornell Road
Cincinnati, Ohio 45242
Tel: (513)489-7600
Fax: (513)489-9229
www.evercoat.com

Finesse Tape Products
PO Box 541428
Linden Hill Station
Flushing NY 11354
800 228 1258
718 939 8837
www.finessepinstriping.com

House of Kolor
Division of Valspar Refinish
210 Crosby St.
Picayune MS 39466
Tech-line: 601 798 4229
houseofkolor@valspar.com

Kirby's Custom Paint
Precision Paint Removers
2415 W Ind Blvd, Bay 1
Long Lake,  MN 55356
952 476 4545

Kosmoski, Jon
House of Kolor Inc
800 844 4130 voice mail box

National Detroit
PO Box 2285
Rockford, IL 61131
815 877 4941
nationaldetroit@compuserve.com

ParaLite
ww.fullspectrumsolutions.com

Protools and Equipment
Spray booths and equipment
23529 Eacles Nest Rd
Antioch, IL 60002
800 989 3747

Sid Moses
Pinstriping brushes
800 628 2194
310 475 1111
sid@moscart.com

Spray Shield Industries
1430 North Seventh St.
Murphysboro, IL. 62966
Phone : 1-888-883-4583
Fax : 1-618-684-8822

System One
www.systemoneproducts.com